Two Horizons

A Memoir of Travel and Transformation

Robert Goluba

Evertouch Publishing

Copyright © 2021 by Robert Goluba

Published in the United States by Evertouch Publishing, an imprint of Evertouch Inc.

Gilbert, Arizona

ISBN 978-1-7330513-5-4 (Print)

All rights reserved. This book is a work of nonfiction based on the author's notes and memory. Some names and identifying details have been changed. No part of this book may be reproduced in any form or by any electronic or mechanical means, including information storage and retrieval systems, without permission in writing from the publisher, except by a reviewer, who may quote brief passages in a review.

Edited by Rachel Small

Cover Design by MiblArt

Contents

1. Chapter 1 — 1
2. Chapter 2 — 9
3. Chapter 3 — 19
4. Chapter 4 — 29
5. Chapter 5 — 35
6. Chapter 6 — 43
7. Chapter 7 — 53
8. Chapter 8 — 61
9. Chapter 9 — 69
10. Chapter 10 — 77
11. Chapter 11 — 83
12. Chapter 12 — 89
13. Chapter 13 — 97
14. Chapter 14 — 101
15. Chapter 15 — 109
16. Chapter 16 — 117
17. Chapter 17 — 125

18. Chapter 18	133
19. Chapter 19	141
20. Chapter 20	149
21. Chapter 21	157
22. Chapter 22	165
23. Chapter 23	177
24. Chapter 24	185
25. Chapter 25	193
26. Chapter 26	201
27. Chapter 27	207
About Author	209

Chapter 1

An armful of cheap souvenirs and a slew of bad memories comprised my haul from my first adventure outside the United States. It was a quick jaunt to Tijuana, and at twelve years old, I experienced many firsts on that warm summer's day. It was the first time I saw a teenage boy paid to look after our car while my family and I shopped at the outdoor markets. It was my first encounter with the barter system pervasive in tourist areas throughout Mexico. And it was the first time I locked eyes with a rat so huge I assumed it was another stray dog.

I'd just completed a masterful negotiation with a street vendor for a brown sombrero larger than my seven-year-old sister, as I was determined not to leave without obnoxious evidence of my first international excursion. The sombrero's silver and gold beads glistening in the sun, I put it on and leaned against a horseless carriage tourists could take pictures with. That's when I made eye contact with the rat. I swear it shot me a sinister grin, and I sensed it was planning an ambush. I froze. I couldn't yell or run. Nobody else seemed to notice the gray monster lurking between the curb and the carriage, and I couldn't warn them.

After what seemed like an eternity, my mom noticed I was uncharacteristically quiet. She stared at me for a few seconds, then scanned the area for the source of the fear plastered on my face. She must have seen the rat, because she turned in a flash, grabbed my sister's hand, and marched our family of five back to the parking lot to retrieve our vehicle. I hadn't wanted to go to Mexico in the first place, and my resentment only grew as we eased into a spot among the twenty lanes of vehicles waiting at the border crossing. I stewed in the back seat of our rental car until we finally crossed back into the United States two hours later.

The Tijuana excursion had been a last-minute decision during a visit with my aunt and cousins in Southern California. I'd recently recovered from air sickness—I'd thrown up from Albuquerque to Anaheim on the flight from Chicago to California. It had been my first flight, and I'd hated it. My nausea subsided only after a couple of days of beach therapy in Carlsbad and Oceanside, about thirty minutes north of San Diego, so leaving the beach to haggle with street vendors hadn't exactly been an appealing idea. My opinion didn't matter because my aunt had thought we'd all have a ball. She claimed to be a regular visitor to Tijuana and raved about it, but looking back, I'm certain she wished to get back at my dad for something he'd done to her growing up. Knowing my aunt, we should have seen this coming, but my dad took the bait, and hours later, we crossed and cemented my first impression of international travel.

The adventure in Mexico confirmed the belief I'd already formed in my young mind—it wasn't necessary to leave the good ol' US of A. I had no desire to do it again, especially after having filled a barf bag multiple times on an airplane. Not only did I not know about other cultures, but I also didn't care. Driving to another country had been dreadful enough, but flying over the ocean to visit a foreign land? That was the definition of insanity to me.

I returned to my hometown of Streator, Illinois, sporting tan and blond highlights in my dark-caramel hair to prove I didn't just go on vacation, but that I went to California. Two weeks later, summer break ended, and I resumed my position as the runt of the class. At less than five feet and one hundred pounds, I was the smallest boy in seventh grade, and all but a few girls in my class towered over me. Despite my diminutive size, bullying wasn't typically a problem for me. Although I was tiny, I was fast—and I wasn't above using that speed to avoid getting pummeled. I'd loiter around the popular kids to the point where a stranger might mistake me for part of the group. It worked as long as I was quiet or didn't make any sudden moves to draw attention to my presence. I thought the boys on the school basketball team were the coolest on the planet, and I wanted nothing more than to be accepted into their clan.

Then something amazing happened after my thirteenth birthday that fall. I'd grown a couple inches since my last birthday, and I was still growing. When I turned fourteen, I'd grown nine inches in a little over twelve months—and went from the shortest to one of the tallest kids in my class. Suddenly, the boys I once looked up to welcomed me into their group. I was finally accepted, an insider for the first time in my life. I loved it and relished the thought of clawing up several rungs of the social ladder at the start of eighth grade.

It was the mid-eighties, and overall, life was good for my friends and me, especially now that I was one of the guys. I loved everything about living in my small town of fifteen thousand residents, two hours southwest of downtown Chicago.

Streator owes its existence to coal mining and glass-bottle manufacturing—the latter leading world production for a time in the 1960s and 1970s. Many of my friends' parents worked in the glass factory, and you never wanted to get caught drinking a soda from a can in their houses. The population of Streator grew swiftly at the turn of the twentieth century, and immigrants from Eastern Europe arrived to fill the plentiful job vacancies in the labor-intensive industries. Shops and restaurants grew along Main Street, a half-dozen blocks long, to complement the neighborhoods sprouting up in the area. The new buildings formed a community surrounded by miles of corn and soybean fields.

My childhood home was only one mile outside the city limits, but it felt more like an ocean away from civilization. Our two-story house with a homemade basketball hoop hung over the driveway in the middle of a quiet lane with a cul-de-sac at the end. The neighbors across the street had tens of thousands of acres of farmland behind them, and about five hundred feet behind our home was a forest with a creek passing through. My younger brother and sister and I had an endless supply of outdoor entertainment. Several families on my street had kids near my age, and we all explored and played on every inch of property accessible by foot or bike. My next-door neighbor was one of my best friends. He came from a family of outdoor enthusiasts and often invited me to go fishing or hunting. If we weren't on the bank of a body of water or traversing a forest with BB guns, we'd play one-on-one baseball, basketball, or football until it was too dark to see. I loved lying on the warm asphalt road in front of our homes and watching the dark sky in the east devour the lighter sky in the west until the stars arrived to rejoice in their nightly domination of the sky. For hours at a time, we'd lie on the street and talk, dream, and periodically count shooting stars. We moved only to let the occasional car pass or when the tone of our mothers calling us in for the night turned angry.

The day I started high school, I slid hard back down every rung of the social ladder I'd worked so hard to climb two years earlier. I had to navigate the transition from a Catholic K–8 school, where I'd had the same thirty classmates for nine years, to a public high school with two hundred and fifty freshmen who'd all attended the same public junior high school together. Despite these hurdles, I thought I might have an advantage in making new friends—the football team began twice-a-day practices a week before classes started my freshman year, and I planned to use this opportunity to befriend some of my teammates. But my attempts to infiltrate the tight-knit groups of guys from the public junior high failed. Their cliques were impenetrable, and when classes started, I'd still made no new friends.

This turned out to be a blessing. Two friends from my grade school had the same lunch hour as I did, so I spent more time with them and we grew to be best friends. One of them is still a close friend today. Together, we did all the awkward things young men do while trying to find their place in high school. For me, life was about sports, sports, and more sports, with a generous amount of social life sprinkled on top. After football season ended, I stood straight and tall to extend my five-foot, ten-inch frame when I tried out for the basketball team. Despite being shorter than all but one other guy trying out and my inability to dribble or shoot very well, I made the team. Fortunately, I attended one of the ten high schools in the country that valued my ability to take elbows to the face to secure a rebound and keep the bench warm for the starters a few minutes each game.

For my first two years of high school, I played football in the fall, basketball in the winter, and baseball for the city league in the spring. I quit playing basketball after my sophomore year and traded my baseball mitt for track cleats my junior and senior years. I never excelled at any of those sports, and I probably tarnished my family name on multiple occasions. However, my friends were on those teams and that drove me to endure hours of practice and games each week. Being part of a team, or a group of guys, was the most important thing in the world to me at that time.

I considered myself to be of average intelligence unless the topic interested me. If I was interested,

I'd research the intricacies of a compelling topic for hours or even days, which probably inched up my IQ a few points. For example, wild animals have always been interesting to me. On my tenth birthday, I'd received the Wildlife Treasury animal cards in the rigid green box. I studied all 324 of those cards until they were dog-eared and floppy. Today, I still know the gestation period of the three-toed sloth and continue to have nightmares about aye-ayes—the long-fingered, grub-eating primates from Madagascar. Professional athletes and the history of jet airplanes also drew my attention. I loved everything about jets except flying in them, which squashed any desire to be a pilot at an early age.

Cultures outside my small Midwestern town and circle of friends, on the other hand, weren't even in the same room as my interests. This wasn't due to a lack of effort by my parents. They often showed me worlds that existed beyond the city limits of Streator. They regularly took my siblings and me to the big city of Chicago to visit museums, attend sporting events, and visit family. We also took annual road trips to see grandparents, cousins, and aunts and uncles in Florida, but none of that sparked an interest in the big world outside Streator. I was more concerned with navigating the constant shifts in social status. In the unwritten and unseen social hierarchy of boys in Streator, I'd been at the bottom rung of the ladder twice, and I didn't want to revisit that position again. I spent my energy trying to find a pickup game of basketball, a party, a car without a leaking radiator, and a job. I even dared to think a girlfriend might be a possibility. Everything seemed possible as long as I stayed within my geographic and social boundaries.

After I celebrated my sixteenth birthday, I put my new driver's license in my wallet, purchased a crappy car, and landed a job flipping burgers. The 1977 Ford Granada sedan had over one hundred and twenty thousand miles on it and a hole in the floorboard large enough to let through several dollars in change as involuntary tolls. The radiator also had a slow leak that left me stranded more than once, but the vehicle had cost me only four hundred dollars, and it ran...most of the time. That was enough for me.

That year, I also got my first girlfriend, so I was walking tall down the school halls. I had everything I needed in life: parents, siblings, good friends, a car, a paycheck, and a girl by my side—at least until someone better asked her out. I was happy living in my safe and slow-paced bubble hidden within the shadows of the tall corn in Central Illinois. I had no desire and no reason to care about anything else...until I did.

Chapter 2

For reasons I can't explain, the study of World War I in history class didn't interest me, but I found everything related to World War II mesmerizing. I suspect it might have been the relative recency of the attack on Pearl Harbor and the D-Day invasion of Normandy, still fresh on the lips and minds of grandparents who'd witnessed those events four decades earlier. Halfway through my junior year in high school, my class dove in deep and studied the countries, presidents, generals, battles, and peace treaties of World War II.

Aside from its role in World War II, Europe might as well have been a dystopian colony of bleeding lepers on the dark side of the moon for all I cared. It wasn't a place I wanted to visit or waste valuable brain cells thinking about, but I did wonder what made the governments, armies, and people of the countries involved do what they did before, during, and after the war. The people of the regions where the bullets flew, bombs exploded, and tanks rumbled especially interested me. How had they endured living through such atrocities right outside their front doors—that is, if their homes still stood? It was hard to fathom those events had occurred a little over forty years before my time sitting in high school history class with Coach B. I felt compelled to learn more about those citizens than the textbooks allowed.

Years later, I learned I'm a five on the Enneagram scale, which explains a lot about my past behavior. The Enneagram is a system of personality typing with nine different types associated with a number. The five is the Investigator. We're people who must thoroughly research things that interest us, and that's always been the case for me. How could something like a world war happen? Twice? The pull to learn and know more was like a school bus-sized magnet, and I was a single steel button. I had to know more.

This interest in global events led to me paying more attention to the news. My parents watched the news every evening, and I'd join them in the family room. A major story in the late eighties was the Cold War, and I was introduced to people such as Mikhail Gorbachev and terms like *glasnost* and *perestroika*. I didn't know what those words meant, but I nervously hoped for the end of the Cold War. Then in 1987, President Ronald Reagan stood in front of the Brandenburg Gate in West Berlin, Germany, and famously said "Mr. Gorbachev, tear down this wall" in what we know today as the Berlin Wall Speech. What was this wall the president spoke of?

Over the years, I watched the battle against communism in Europe with passive interest until the revolution in Poland ended communist rule in the summer of 1989. The Chicago news stations covered the events extensively, and my desire for news and information on global affairs grew. I understood I might have a front-row seat to a seismic shift in the

Cold War and could be watching history unfold right before my eyes. On November 9, 1989, it happened. I watched thousands of Germans climb the Berlin Wall on TV. They brought axes and sledgehammers to tear it down—just as President Reagan had ordered two years earlier. I rooted for them with each swing. My empathy swelled for everyone fighting for freedom and a better life across the Atlantic.

During class one day shortly after that, I shared my interest in the fall of the Berlin Wall and my desire to be a writer with a teacher who also oversaw the school yearbook. It was hard for me to be vulnerable and admit I enjoyed writing, but he was very supportive and asked me to write a few paragraphs to memorialize the important global event. I spent weeks writing three paragraphs, and my connection to the Berlin Wall was cemented in the Streator High School Class of 1990 yearbook.

Meanwhile, I actively pondered what I should do with my life. Almost overnight, leaving my small town and experiencing more of the big world beyond the miles of corn and soybean fields became important, borderline critical to me. College hadn't been a top priority before. It wasn't something we often discussed in my house, and my parents didn't pressure me, but now it seemed to be the best opportunity to pursue my yet-determined career path and experience life away from home.

Once I was sure going away to a university was the next step for me, I told my mom. She always had a smile on her face, but when I told her my decision, her smile vanished and wrinkles formed above her eyebrows. I believe she might have sat down to catch her breath before she asked, "You want to go away to college?"

I didn't relish the idea of spending another four to five years in school. After all, I hadn't exactly loved my first twelve. I just knew I wanted more than I could get in Streator, and college seemed to be the easiest short-term path with long-term benefits.

"Are you sure?" she asked. "You haven't talked about a strong interest in college before. Why the sudden change?"

I shrugged. "I just need to get out of here."

She suggested I try out Illinois Valley Community College (IVCC) for a couple of years. "You could live at home," she said, "and we could even help you get a newer car to drive back and forth."

But I knew the hometown that for so many years had provided everything I needed in the world had shrunk and was now too small for me. Now that I knew something better existed beyond the horizon of corn and bean fields, I had to have it.

"I'm not going to IVCC," I said, shaking my head. "I want to live on a college campus. I'll work full-time or take out loans if I have to—whatever it takes to go away to college."

My mom swallowed hard. I glimpsed the concern on her face. "We can help a little, but we can't pay for your college."

"I know. I'll figure something out," I said, and retreated to my room.

From that point on, I refused to consider any alternative that didn't involve my living on a college campus after graduation. For the first eighteen years of my life, I'd watched my dad work weekly swing shifts at a steel mill thirty-five miles from our house. He'd hated it for as long as I could remember, but he did it because it was one of the best jobs available in the area to provide for his family. I hadn't always known I wanted to go to college, but I'd always been 100 percent sure I didn't want to do shift work in a steel mill.

My mom took care of my brother, my sister, and me, which was no simple task. She also worked part-time at a local retailer. I never once went without the basics, and we even got occasional treats, such as central air conditioning after my sister was born, and a VCR a few years after my friends had one. But I also heard the fights. They were always about money. Both of my parents had taken college courses but never received degrees. I hoped to be different. I wanted to get a degree, and I didn't want to worry about money.

First, I explored loans. I did the math and found I didn't like the idea of a mini-mortgage payment waiting for me along with my first paycheck. Then, I considered working at the steel mill with my dad during the summer and saving every penny of the ten-dollar-an-hour wage—back when the minimum wage was still under four bucks an hour. The union positions paid overtime and double time on Sundays, so I figured I could really rack up the hours, but it turned out the plant wasn't hiring any summer help that year. Next, I toyed with the idea of commuting sixty to ninety minutes to one of the state universities for classes every day as a plan B. Some people in Streator drove those distances for work and school all the time, but I couldn't imagine driving that far in the frigid and snowy Illinois winters, so I ruled out daily commuting. I was running out of options.

Along with the colleges and universities, all the military branches were recruiting seniors. I signed up to speak to the Army Reserve recruiter, and after meeting with him in school, I scheduled a time for him to visit with my parents and me at home.

My mom teared up when I told her an Army recruiter was coming over, and my dad yelled at me for upsetting my mom. I'd thought my dad, a Vietnam veteran and former Navy Seabee, would be supportive of my interest in the military. I'd heard for eighteen years I could benefit from the discipline provided by the military, but once he found out an Army recruiter was on his way and the prospect of my joining the military was real, my dad shared that his experience in Vietnam had been a negative one. He told me a couple of stories and said he didn't want me to go through the same thing. My dad had never talked about Vietnam with me before and the stories were jarring, but before I had time to react, a white sedan pulled into our driveway. Moments later, I answered the knock at our door and led the recruiter to our kitchen table.

I told him about my desire to go to college and explained I was interested in their education benefits. He told me about the GI Bill and loan repayment programs. At the time, the GI Bill and monthly drill pay combined provided around three hundred and fifty dollars a month. That was only about twenty-five percent of what I needed each year, but it would get me closer to affording college. The recruiter left after I said I needed time to think about it.

I felt trapped. Almost every day after that, my parents and I argued about whether I should join the Army Reserve. They thought community college for two years was a reasonable compromise. I disagreed. The tension was so thick that during a fight, I almost called the recruiter and signed up on the spot, but common sense prevailed. Nine weeks of basic training and six years of weekend drills once a month was a long commitment just to spite someone.

I leaned toward enlisting, so I reached out to a friend who'd already joined. He'd enlisted when he was a junior and had gone to basic training the summer before his senior year. He explained he planned to attend college and the National Guard would pay for 100 percent of his tuition if he enrolled in a state school.

I was confused. "The Army Reserve won't pay for my tuition in any state. Isn't the Army Reserve and the National Guard the same thing?" I asked.

"The National Guard is similar to the Army Reserve, but it's not the same," my friend explained. "It's the same basic training, and both offer the GI Bill, but the National Guard is part of the state, so that's why they pay tuition to a state school. The Army Reserve is national, so they don't."

The wheels inside my head turned, and smoke practically came out of my ears—going away to college was now within reach. The three hundred and fifty dollars per month could go toward room and board and even some living expenses if the National Guard paid my tuition.

My shortlist of colleges included the University of Iowa, Purdue University, and Illinois State University

(ISU). I wanted to turn my love of writing into an advertising executive role and they all had attractive creative writing or marketing tracts that could lead me to an advertising career after college. As my friend and I talked, ISU in Normal, Illinois, became my top and final choice. I told him I was interested and scheduled a meeting with the Illinois Army National Guard recruiter at home with my parents the following week. This time, I was excited about the meeting. I'd nearly joined the Army Reserve with limited tuition assistance, so the National Guard seemed like a no-brainer.

"You know you don't have to do this," my dad told me the day before the recruiter arrived. "We'll find another way."

I knew my dad wanted to protect me from the negative experience he had in the military, but there hadn't been a war in over twenty years, and the Cold War was over. "I want to join the military," I said. "I think it will be good for me."

My dad turned to my mom, and she nodded. "We'll support your decision if this is what you want to do."

"It is."

The next day, Sergeant Bradley from the Illinois Army National Guard sat at our kitchen table with pamphlets and a black US ARMY binder with information on tuition assistance. Two weeks later, he drove me to the Military Entrance Processing Station in Chicago for a physical. That day, I was officially sworn in as a member of the Illinois Army National Guard.

In my rush to secure tuition assistance, I hadn't asked too many questions. My friend who'd already gone to basic training had made it sound like boy scout camp but with M16 rifles to shoot and live grenades to toss around for fun. That was good enough for me.

One week after my high school graduation ceremony, I boarded a plane and then a bus to Fort Leonard Wood training base in southern Missouri to start basic training. I was about to embark on the most significant transformation of my life.

Chapter 3

Minutes after I arrived at my training unit, Alpha 31st, I was subjected to the only event my friend had warned me about—shakedown. More than a dozen drill sergeants eagerly waited for two hundred and forty new Army privates to get off the transport truck. The moment the doors opened, the barrage of yelling began, and we all pushed our way off. We shuffled to our assigned square on the pavement with our duffel bags. Once all the transport trucks were empty, the drill sergeants divided us into smaller groups on the concrete pavilion in front of our barracks. Shakedown is the process of taking inventory of all newly assigned gear and making it as painful on the new privates as possible. It's where the drill sergeants establish they are in charge, so they shouted at us to do every task faster under the sweltering Missouri sun. It felt as if they outnumbered us despite our twenty-to-one advantage. No matter what anyone did, it was wrong, and the drill sergeants roared louder.

The drill sergeant for my group looked like Tom Cruise—same height and smile. He stood in silence and watched the troops in his section respond to the Sergeant First Class's commands.

"Hold up your canteen with your left hand. Now hold up your ammo belt with your right hand, and you better not let your duffel bag hit the pavement," the Sergeant First Class barked.

My arms burned, but I followed along exactly as instructed and chuckled at the thought I might skate through the shakedown my friend told me had been a living hell for him. The Tom Cruise-clone drill sergeant saw my lips curve up for a nanosecond and was on me faster than a stray dog on a steak bone.

His round brown hat repeatedly hit my forehead so hard it left fabric marks on my skin, all while his spittle covered my neck, chin, and cheeks. He made me drop into the push-up position on the hot pavement, where I stayed until my arms felt as if they'd spontaneously combust. Then he made me do it again. And then a third time. I remember thinking the drill sergeants would have to stop after a few hours because they couldn't keep up that level of intensity all day—I was used to football practice, where the coaches pushed to bend you. I'd never been so wrong. These drill sergeants had no desire to bend us. They were there to break each of us down to our core, and they weren't leaving until they'd completed the mission.

Later that evening, after all the squawking finally subsided, I stood in line for dinner chow, still in shock. I was deeply concerned I wouldn't survive another eighty-four days in that pressure-cooker environment and questioned my decision to go away to college and join the military. Like every other soldier in the mess hall, I ate my meal in silence and without looking up in less than five minutes. The drill sergeants had said if we looked up from our food, we must be done eating. I heard a few people dismissed seconds after sitting, and I didn't want to add hunger to my long list of concerns that day.

After dinner, we marched around the base for another couple of hours and finally retreated to our barracks fourteen hours after arriving. This certainly wasn't how I'd wanted to start basic training. Before arriving at Fort Leonard Wood, I'd thought the training would be a good personal challenge—that this wasn't just an opportunity to pay for college, but also an opportunity to prove to myself I could do something really, really hard. I didn't want to just survive; I wanted to thrive. Except my voice was hoarse, my head was pounding, and my legs were cramping. I was terrified I'd fail, and I wasn't alone.

Every soldier in my room was physically exhausted and emotionally beaten. A few guys broke down crying. I heard "Why?" and "I want to go home" between the sobs. After the crying stopped, the room remained silent until one brave soul asked: "Anyone else worried that you won't be able to make it through basic training after today?"

That's all it took. Eight strangers shared their deepest fears and concerns. We commiserated over the worst day of our young lives, and bonds formed. At that moment, I knew my fellow trainees, especially my battle buddy on the bunk above me, were the only way I'd make it through basic training.

As the weeks went on, the heat, lack of sleep, and constant berating from the drill sergeants overwhelmed me, but the pressure eased a little each day. Eventually, basic training became tolerable. Meanwhile, the bonds with my roommates and the other seventy-five men on the second floor that made up the second platoon of Alpha company grew. For the first time in my life, I was surrounded by people who weren't my family and my friends from home. I hadn't been one of those small-town kids holed up inside the compound of a cult leader or trapped on the side of a distant mountain, miles from the real world, but I hadn't had a personal relationship with anyone culturally different from me. At Fort Leonard Wood, I became fast friends with my Hispanic and African American roommates. I met Native Americans for the first time and people of the Jewish, Muslim, and Mormon faiths.

There were several prolific storytellers in my platoon. Most of their stories made me laugh, while others made me want to punch a wall or even cry. I wanted to learn more about the men behind these stories. On Sundays, we had a couple of hours of free time after the Catholic, Protestant, and Jewish soldiers attended their church services while the others stayed behind and cleaned the barracks. During this free time, a dozen or more guys would commonly cram into a room and discuss race, religion, politics, and other topics often considered taboo. Accounts of older brothers getting shot by rival gang members, of cousins overdosing on the reservation, of parents getting separated from children by border patrol, and of families with eight kids who didn't drink coffee, soda, or beer were shared in those rooms.

In every conversation, I learned things I don't think I would've learned anywhere else. There was something unique and extraordinary about everyone wearing the same uniform and going through hell together. It was a common thread among us, no matter what race or religion was under those olive-drab pants, shirts, and caps, and it was a strong one. We discussed stereotypes and myths and joked with each other. The conversations were fun yet informative. I grew to love and respect my new friends, and by the time I'd finished basic training, I was ready and willing to take a bullet for any of them. I guess those drill sergeants knew what they were doing after all.

After basic training, I started my Advanced Individual Training (AIT) to become a combat engineer. All combat engineers required four weeks of training on land mines and explosives such as TNT and C-4. I wish I could share a riveting story about why I chose to become a combat engineer over all the other options, but it was mainly because the National Guard Armory was near my parents' house and I thought blowing things up without getting in trouble sounded fun. AIT was less rigid than basic training, but the drill sergeants' attitude changed from semi-relaxed to stressed at the end of the first week. Trucks, tanks, armored personnel carriers, and Humvees parked on the lot near my barracks received paint jobs, going from jungle camouflage to the color of sand. Nobody knew what was going on outside our little corner of

Fort Leonard Wood, but I sensed it wasn't good. Then, a couple of days later, the drill sergeants told us we were going to war with Iraq and we'd be shifting from training during a time of peace to training for combat. I thought about what I'd told my dad about there being no wars in my lifetime. My lucky streak was about to end. The first Gulf War, known as Desert Shield, was brewing and this left me with mixed emotions. On the one hand, I was fond of my limbs and hoped to celebrate my twentieth birthday without the physical or mental scars of war. On the other hand, I felt prepared for combat after months of intense training and didn't want to let down my Army brothers. I remember it felt kind of like sitting on the bench during a basketball game in high school. I was apprehensive about being good enough to be on the court, but the drive to support my teammates was greater. Despite my doubts, I still wanted to be in the arena with my teammates and the same applied to the battlefield.

AIT soon became just as intense as basic training. I took my training seriously, given that I might be using my new skills soon. Fifteen weeks after my last day of high school, I graduated from Army basic training and AIT. I got to go home with the others in the Army Reserves and National Guard, but my roommates in the regular Army were deployed to their overseas stations. One roommate left for South Korea, while three others flew to Germany to join their new units before deploying to the Middle East. Now I was interested and concerned about areas throughout the United States and around the world. I studied up on Kuwait and Iraq and the tumultuous history in the

Middle East. Our country was on the brink of war, so I had little choice but to keep my eyes and ears open to the global crisis. This caused me to mature quickly. Focusing solely on myself and hiding in the relative obscurity of my hometown was no longer an option.

Once I returned home, I had a little over a hundred days to prepare for another dramatic change in my life. I'd be switching from the intense structure of basic training to the freedom of campus life at Illinois State University. I took a couple of weeks to decompress and adjust physically and mentally to civilian life again. After that, I worked at a local big box store and prepared for college while keeping my eye on the news to find out if the Gulf War had escalated enough to send more ground troops. The Army activated several National Guard units to backfill the regular Army units whose soldiers had been deployed to the Middle East. I knew it was possible if the United States entered an extended ground war, I might have to trade a dorm room for a bunk bed at an Army base in Georgia, Oklahoma, or Texas. If the conflict continued, my sleeping quarters could be in the back of an armored personnel carrier in the Middle East.

Christmas and New Year's Day passed, and the Gulf War was still mainly an air assault by the US Air Force and the Navy, so I packed for ISU. My parents helped me move into my coed dorm, and I met my new roommate, Bill. He was a nice-enough dude and was always respectful of my personal property and space—two things not always as common as they should be among college roommates.

My first semester at ISU reminded me of life in my hometown. Most of the people who lived on my floor were also middle-class white kids from small towns, and we all clicked right away. We went to the cafeteria next to my dorm for lunch and dinner every day and crashed parties together on weekends. While other freshmen on my floor got caught up in the social scene, I had powerful motivation to succeed academically. The National Guard only paid for courses in which you received a grade of C or better. Knowing you'd gone through hell—and potentially might be shipped off to war—just to attend college was a great motivator to never, ever fail.

Some students would go out at night and blow off classes the next day. I liked to go out too, but I made a rule for myself: I had to complete my studies before I could go out. It worked. After getting mostly Bs and Cs with an occasional A in high school, I saw more As and achieved the highest GPA of my life after my first semester in college.

When I returned to ISU in the fall, it was a different experience. The threat of the Gulf War had subsided, and I still lived with Bill, but a more diverse group of people now lived on our floor. There was a common area between the male suites and the female suites, with couches arranged in a horseshoe shape. On any given night, I could walk out of my room and join a discussion or debate in the common area. I loved to mix things up with this new crew of floormates and spent hours discussing current events. Although I'd formed new beliefs with exposure to people who were different from me in terms of race, religion, and sexual orientation, I still held my personal convictions from growing up in a small town. That made for some lively discussions. They weren't quite as honest and raw as the discussions I'd engaged in during basic training, but close.

The second half of 1991 and the first half of 1992 provided ample material for discussion. Clarence Thomas became the second African American Supreme Court justice, Magic Johnson announced he had HIV, and the Cold War officially ended after President Mikhail Gorbachev resigned and the Soviet Union dissolved. Countries were adopting democracy, and Berlin celebrated its first anniversary as the new capital of Germany.

The famous wall in the German capital city had always loomed in the shadows of my life. And soon, it was going to come out of the background and affect my life in a way I'd never imagined.

Chapter 4

After my first two semesters in college, I'd accumulated a strong GPA and was oozing with confidence. College courses were less complicated than I'd expected, and I was getting better grades than I'd envisioned, so I pushed all my chips into the middle of the table. I came up with the bright idea to take all my most challenging courses in one semester to get them out of the way. The plan was to endure four months of stormy seas in exchange for smooth sailing until graduation. Not seeing a downside to my plan, I signed up for accounting, calculus, statistics, and a foreign language course. I'd taken two years of Spanish in high school and had a rudimentary understanding of the Latin language, but I chose German as my college-level foreign language.

When friends asked why I chose German over Spanish, I was already questioning my decision and tired of defending my choices, so I replied I didn't know to end the conversation. The truth was I felt a connection to Germany and its people after witnessing the divided nation I'd grown up knowing as two different countries reunited as one unified Germany. A sliver of this connection might have been the German DNA passed down from my maternal grandmother, but I was just as much French, Irish, and Slovak as German. The genuine connection came from the article I wrote in my senior yearbook. Those three paragraphs would forever link me to Germany.

The new year arrived, and I was ready for a semester with my nose to the grindstone. Two days after I returned to campus, though, my plans changed. Three friends who lived on my floor, Steve, Aaron, and Marc, wanted to join a fraternity. Steve and Aaron were freshmen and determined to do so, while Marc and I were starting our second year on campus, so we went along to see what the hoopla was all about. As it turned out, all four of us decided we liked the same group of guys and submitted our pledges to that fraternity. We were all accepted and became members of the Sigma Alpha Epsilon fraternity—or SAE, as it was more commonly known on campus. Pledging a fraternity was like a part-time job on top of my ambitious class schedule.

My first day in German class was a rude awakening. A woman in her late twenties with fair skin and thin, stringy hair paced in front of the room while speaking German. I looked around and saw heads bobbing. The other students appeared to understand her. After a few minutes, I gathered her name was Frau Becker and she wanted us to reply with our names. The other students spoke to her in German, and their names were the only words I understood. Then she looked in my direction. I pointed at my chest to confirm she was indeed talking to me to buy one more second of time before embarrassing myself.

"Hi, my name is Rob, and I don't know any German."

"Nein, nein, nein. Sprich Deutsch," she replied, which means, "No, no, no. Speak in German."

I shrugged. "I don't know what you just said."

Frau Becker took a long look at me and leaned against the whiteboard. "This is going to be the last time you hear me speak English. This is a class to learn German, so we will speak only German during class. I realize some of you are farther along than others, but full immersion is the only way you'll learn in the short time I have to work with you."

The class ended, and I left troubled but not deterred. I still had accounting, statistics, and calculus to contend with, so German class was only twenty-five percent of my problem. And as the semester continued, German became the least of my concerns. Calculus felt far more like a foreign language to me, and insufficient time-management skills reared their ugly heads. I skipped class or much-needed study time to attend fraternity functions in order to avoid a tongue-lashing from the pledge leader. I began drowning in poor grades and didn't see any way I could succeed at everything. A month before finals, I was struggling to pass any of my classes.

A significant portion of the German class was about history and culture. It turned out there was more to German history than two world wars and a psychopath with a toothbrush mustache. It intrigued me. German customs, politics, beer, architecture, religion, music, healthcare, food, and philosophies caught my attention, so in typical Investigator fashion, I studied them in depth. I often looked up from my textbook and wondered what it would be like to live in Germany and experience their culture firsthand.

Meanwhile, life outside my safe, insulated college campus got more complicated. Perhaps I'd just become more aware of things, but it felt as if extraordinary circumstances were popping up regularly in the news cycles in the first half of 1992. The end of the conflict in Iraq, a struggling post-recession economy, and a looming presidential election dominated the headlines.

While I studied late into the night to pull up my grades, the world waited for the verdict of four LAPD officers caught on camera beating a man named Rodney King, an African American man they pulled over for a traffic violation. A low hum of tension permeated the campus during the trial, and I likened it to a shaken soda can ready to burst. Finally, in April 1992, the four officers were acquitted of any crimes.

A wave of disbelief washed over the nation, and massive riots broke out in Los Angeles. More protests and rioting sprung up in cities across America. Soon, even my college town of Normal, Illinois—known more for productive corn and soybean farms than social activism—erupted in protests. Several of the African American students living on my floor took part in the protests. They returned that night to see the entire floor gathered in the common area discussing the riots. For hours, they told stories, and the rest of us asked questions that revealed an America I didn't know or want to believe still existed. I sat, listened, and practiced empathy to better understand a world mostly unknown to me before that day.

At this point, I was two weeks from finals and had to make a tough decision. My original plan for the semester fell apart the day I pledged a fraternity, and now it seemed as if the whole world was as chaotic as my life. It was impossible for me to focus on any one thing, let alone overwhelming courses. I didn't see any way I could study enough to pass all four classes. It was too late to drop out of the fraternity because the damage had already been done. Plus, I liked my fraternity brothers and, similar to my loyalty to my Army brothers, I didn't want to let them down. Among my courses, German was my favorite, so I chose to sacrifice calculus in order to have time to study for the other three. I'd never had a C in college, and I was facing a sure F in my attempt to get at least a C in the other three courses. The bad news was my plan worked—I got my other three grades up to a C and received an F in Calculus. I had nothing to show for a class I'd struggled in for three months and would have to retake. I felt sick and defeated.

As a rule, I try not to dwell on the past, and I have few regrets in life, but I feel nothing but disappointment when I think of the first half of 1992. Two solid semesters of college made me overconfident. I knew better but still piled on one poor decision after another that year in my attempt to outsmart the recommended path for my degree. Focused on wanting to enjoy leisurely junior and senior years, I'd tried to buck the system and it had bucked me right back, knocking me to the ground.

After the semester from hell was over, I returned home to Streator for the summer and worked in the hot and noisy steel mill with my dad. I was able to make enough money to save for college, and it wasn't too stressful. It was the wisest decision I made that year.

Chapter 5

I returned to the ISU campus in the fall of 1992 a humbled man. My once-respectable GPA had plummeted to my high school average, and I was on academic probation with the fraternity. After significant time invested as a pledge, I risked getting kicked out of the fraternity if I duplicated the results of my previous semester.

Despite my argument that I'd never need calculus for a career in marketing, the university told me I had to retake calculus or change my major from marketing to a nonbusiness degree. I didn't have a plan B for a major, and calculus still seemed like a foreign language to me, so this time I took the opposite approach and stacked the easiest courses still available to me. I had to focus all my attention on calculus to pass.

During that semester, I settled into my new apartment on campus with friends, took an officer position with the fraternity, and studied regularly. Thankfully, though I still didn't understand calculus, I understood just enough to get a C. I clawed back about half of the GPA I'd lost the previous semester after receiving As in my other courses. I'd learned my lesson: Don't try to game the system. Simply take a balanced load of classes and study for all of them.

The previous semester now felt like a lifetime ago. I'd nearly forgotten the small amount of German I could speak six months earlier. Although my interest in German culture was still high, my opportunities to do anything beyond ordering a bottle of imported German beer were nonexistent. Another year passed, and I doubted I'd ever need to speak German again—until a poster in the student center stopped me in my tracks.

The colorful ad was for an informational meeting regarding a study abroad program. The ad featured an image of a traditional German neighborhood with ornate two- and three-story half-timber homes with gable roofs huddled around a city square. Multiple colleges and countries were available through the program. My eyes moved down the list of destinations until I reached the bullet point I'd hoped to find—the University of Paderborn, in Germany. I'd never heard of Paderborn, and I didn't know where it was located in relation to Berlin, Frankfurt, or Munich. The only thing I was sure of was Paderborn was in Germany, and that was good enough for me. Eighteen months after my last German 101 class, my interest in the newly unified Germany was rekindled.

On the day of the informational meeting, I arrived early to get a seat at the front of the auditorium. The presenter introduced himself as Professor Carlson, and he clicked his mouse to project his laptop onto the white screen. For the next thirty minutes, he shared images of all the destinations available. Spain, Norway, and Australia also looked like attractive options, but

I focused on the German slides. My heart beat faster with each picture of former study abroad students in Berlin, Cologne, and Paderborn. Next, another professor took the clicker, and she provided the dates and durations of each program. The study abroad program in Paderborn, Germany, started in six months, on May 26, 1994, and lasted four weeks. We'd each live with a participating host family near the university and attend classes on campus. Some host families would take up to two students if we had a travel buddy who was also part of the study abroad program.

For the rest of the presentation, my knees bounced and my feet tapped the floor. The chance to fully immerse myself in German culture was closer than I'd ever expected.

My elation waned as the full weight of the situation grew clear, though. I would be flying across the Atlantic to live in a foreign country. How would I pay for it? Did I feel comfortable traveling over five thousand miles away for a month by myself? Could I get permission from the National Guard to miss one, or possibly two, weekend drills? Would I like the food?

I staggered back to my room at the fraternity house, exhausted from the dueling emotions inside my head. I spun the leather band around my wrist a dozen times while I lay in bed that night staring at the ceiling. Despite the cold temperature outside, I felt overheated lying on top of my comforter.

The next day, I approached a fraternity brother known for his penchant for adventure. Before finally falling asleep the previous night, I'd decided finding a travel partner would be the best way to ease my anxiety.

Scott and I were good friends, and I felt he was my best shot.

I swallowed hard and made my pitch. "Hey, Scott, I just went to a meeting about this really cool study abroad program in Germany. It's only four weeks long, and we get to go to a college campus and visit cities like Cologne and Berlin. We'd live with a host family and get six credit hours for those four weeks. I'm going to go and wanted to see if anyone else wants to go."

"I have relatives from Germany—I'll go," Scott replied, as if I'd just asked if he wanted pepperoni or mushrooms on his pizza.

"So you really want to go?"

"Yeah, I've always wanted to check it out."

"Do you need to check with your parents or anything?"

"Nah, I'm good. Count me in."

His quick response and commitment despite not knowing many details or how to speak German shocked me, but I was relieved. Now that I had a travel companion, I could work on my parents and the National Guard.

The US military was a cakewalk compared to my parents. The commanding officer agreed to let me make up my weekend drills as long as I completed the required days before my trip. Easy peasy. I lost the battle of the financial discussion with my parents before it even started. By this time, my brother was a sophomore at ISU, and my sister was a senior in high school and also had plans to attend ISU in the fall, so money was tight. My best option was to take out a loan.

During my first three years at ISU, I'd resisted taking out student loans—a source of great pride for me. I'd done the math, though, and wouldn't be able to earn the forty-five hundred dollars needed for the study abroad program, airfare, and incidentals by the deadline. I agonized over the decision for weeks, but the chance to study and live in Germany was too alluring. Just before the deposit deadline, I completed the paperwork and received a four-thousand-dollar student loan. It was enough to cover the flight and the extra fees and tuition the National Guard wouldn't pay, but it left little for spending money. I was used to pinching pennies to get by as a college student, so I figured I'd just have to do the same in Europe.

I spent hours over the next five months preparing for the most extensive trip I'd ever taken. After securing my passport, booking my flight, and purchasing a calling card, I read books on how to travel through Europe on a budget. I purchased a Eurail pass that would allow me to travel anywhere in Europe by train, and Scott and I pored over the study abroad program itinerary and carved out one weekend for a trip to Paris and another to Munich.

Once all my arrangements were finalized, I counted down the days until May 25. On the morning of the flight, my stomach was already experiencing turbulence. The third or fourth flight of my life would be an eight-hour hop across the pond, from Chicago to Frankfurt. I had flashbacks to my full barf bag a decade earlier, but I told myself at least it was a direct flight, so it would be over sooner.

Scott and I arrived at O'Hare International Airport in Chicago and stepped up to the counter to show our passports with the confidence of seasoned overseas travelers. The woman behind the computer typed for a few seconds, then stated the flight was overbooked. She offered us a connecting flight through London to Frankfurt and noted it would arrive in Frankfurt within fifteen minutes of our original flight, so we had nothing to lose. Of course, she wasn't aware I might lose my lunch right there on her counter upon hearing this news. I stared back in disbelief. My stomach churned, and my chest tightened. Was this a sign? Should I turn around and bolt for the door?

While I pondered my next move, the employee added the airline would give us each a two-hundred-dollar voucher for a future flight if we took the voluntary bump to the connecting flight. Scott looked at me and raised his eyebrows. I shook my head. Scott, always the negotiator, winked at me and turned back to the woman. He said he'd do it if they gave him two hundred in cold hard cash. I told my nerves to pound sand and said I'd also be interested in cash. After a couple of phone calls, the airline agreed.

On board, I found my middle seat among the middle seats. There were five seats on my right and five seats on my left in our row on the United Airlines wide-body jet. I had the company of a crying baby on one side and a drunk, snoring cowboy on the other. A dose of Dramamine prevented a repeat of air sickness and also made me drowsy. Although I desperately wanted to fall asleep, I think I was the only person who didn't sleep on that leg of our journey. It was too uncomfortable, and

I was too excited to do any more than close my eyes and relax. It was a relief to land at London's Heathrow Airport, where Scott and I caught the Lufthansa flight to Frankfurt.

Everything about my journey to Germany changed as soon as the Frankfurt-based Lufthansa flight attendants shut the cabin door. The announcements were in German, and the captain jerked the Airbus jet away from the bridge right on time. My German professor had pounded into our heads that Germans were very punctual, and that we could miss planes and trains if we were even a minute late. I believed her now.

The plane taxied toward the runway while several passengers stood and messed with their overhead luggage. A flight attendant told the last man still standing to sit down because the plane was about to take off, but he continued rearranging something in his suitcase. Seconds later, the aircraft turned onto the runway, and the thrust pushed me deep into the seat. I looked over my shoulder at the man who'd been standing seconds earlier—he was now lying in the aisle several rows back, his arms flailing to stop his slide to the rear of the plane. He caught himself, crawled back to his assigned seat, and buckled himself in faster than I'd ever seen. The flight attendants chatted with each other as though it had never happened. This was the German experience I'd been seeking!

Chapter 6

Two hours later, I set foot on mainland Europe for the first time in my life. The airport looked like every other I'd been in, and it was impossible to tell if the pilot had landed the plane in Frankfurt, Germany, or Frankfort, Kentucky—until I noticed the AUSFARHT (exit) sign.

Not sure where to go, Scott and I followed the crowd, and I was excited to be fully immersed in a bustling German transportation hub. We found Lufthansa's customer service area, where we collected our bounty of $200 for taking the bump in Chicago and I received my first crisp deutsche mark bills with colorful images of men and women on the front and German objects on the back. I arranged them neatly in my wallet, and then Scott and I set out to find our study abroad group.

I took in the German signage, the shops with German goods for sale, and the locals going about their business as I strolled through the airport. It was almost as if they didn't know a new American was on their soil with his head spinning in excitement and confusion. As a marketing major, I particularly liked examining the ads. They were all fun, bold, and interesting. My face turned bright red and I put my hand over my mouth like an embarrassed toddler at the sight of magazine covers with topless women on racks outside the newsstand.

At the designated meeting area, Scott and I found our study abroad student advisor, Professor Carlson, and his wife. We followed them out of the airport doors into a new world. A shuttle bus took us to a hotel near downtown Frankfurt. After checking in to our shared room, Scott and I dropped our luggage and explored our new surroundings. We opened and closed the curtains and turned the sink faucet on and off, but the toilet won our full attention. At that time, German toilets had a "shelf" in the bowl. There was only a small opening with water at the front. Scott found it first. "Check this out—no splashback." I ran over as if he'd just announced he'd found a new animal species and stared at the toilet.

"I can't wait to use it," I replied.

Scott continued to gaze at the toilet, so I tapped him on the shoulder. "Let's go explore."

"Okay, but first I want to try it. I'll be ready in ten minutes."

We soon hit the streets of Frankfurt. After an hour of window shopping, I started noticing all the double takes and long stares we were getting from the locals. Scott was tall and had shoulder-length dreadlocks in his sandy-blond hair. He'd gotten into a fistfight days before our trip and had a cut on his nose and two matching black eyes that made him look like a giant raccoon. At five feet, ten inches tall, I was a half-foot shorter than Scott. I wore my baseball cap backward over my high and tight military-style haircut. We stood out as Americans even among streets full of Americans. I was shocked at the number of times a stranger approached Scott to ask him, in English, what had happened to his eyes. I sensed they were wary of him.

I didn't have much to go on, but my first impression of Germany wasn't a good one. Frankfurt seemed like a typical large American city but much more expensive and with rude citizens. The one person I stopped and asked for directions from yelled at me in broken English to stop speaking with an accent. I told her I didn't know how to speak English any other way, and she stormed off mumbling something in German. I had deutsche marks in my pocket and was walking on streets with signs in German, but I didn't feel I was getting the authentic German experience I'd envisioned for the past six months. I wondered if I'd made a colossal mistake flying five thousand miles to stay with a family I'd never met in a country where I couldn't speak the local language well.

Scott and I went back to our hotel and rested until the rest of the ISU students arrived on a later flight. There were a dozen American students plus Professor Carlson and his wife in the German study abroad program. Once the entire group was intact, Professor Carlson led us like a shepherd to our charter bus. I tossed my duffel bag in the cargo hold and found a seat next to a window. The bus made its way through Frankfurt and then onto the autobahn to our destination two hours north. The sour taste left my mouth like air from a small hole in a balloon as the concrete and steel of Frankfurt transitioned to rolling hills dotted with leafy trees and quaint German villages. The countryside resembled what I'd seen of Wisconsin, yet it was like nothing I'd ever seen. I pushed my face closer to the window to observe as much as possible.

Two hours later, the bus driver guided us off the highway and into a resort in the town of Bergstadt. I stepped down into the parking lot, scanned the area, and inhaled deeply. The scent of maple in the humid air tickled my nose. Any negative impressions of Germany were now long gone.

Professor Carlson ushered the twelve of us into the four-story resort nestled in the wooded hills. After we received our keys, we were instructed to get settled in our two-person rooms and then gather in the lobby. This was our opportunity to meet the German students who were part of the study abroad program. All the students from Germany had plans to attend ISU for the fall semester, and we'd spend a lot of time with them over the summer.

Christian was the first German student I met. He was tall and slender and wore thick-rimmed glasses. He asked, "Sprechen sie Deutsch?" ("Do you speak German"), and I wasn't sure how to respond. Though "nein" ("no") would have been the correct answer, I was eager to see if a real German could understand me, so I gave it a shot. I launched into a few phrases I remembered from my German class and watched wrinkles multiply on Christian's forehead. He didn't appear to understand anything I was trying to say, but he was polite and patient while I struggled to find words and phrases he might understand. Finally, I gave up and told him, "Ich spreche kein Deutsch" ("I do not speak German").

He finally understood me, but then a puzzled look formed on his face, which I could only assume was the result of the question that would have been on my mind: Why come to a university in a foreign country without a basic understanding of the language? My confidence was shot, and I didn't want to attempt speaking German anymore. I'd forgotten most of what I once knew, and it was clear the Germans didn't understand the few phrases I thought I'd mastered. "Ich spreche kein Deutsch" became the most valuable German phrase for me that summer.

Christian and I moved to a larger group nearby. He introduced me to Kristoff, Paul, Suzanne, and Saf, and I introduced him to the American students. The German students asked if I spoke German, and I told them about my collapsed confidence. I gathered that they wanted me to try, but I couldn't muster the courage to continue humiliating myself, so I promised I'd try in the future. Again, they were gracious about the promise and spoke English to me so we could continue to communicate. At the time, I didn't understand why they didn't just speak English if they knew how. I'd come to learn why later in my trip.

We also met Dan, the German students' advisor, and he immediately radiated stereotypical German-villain vibes—the kind you might see in late-night B movies. Dan talked slower than anyone I'd met in the American South, and he shook my hand longer than I felt comfortable with. His bushy, unkempt mustache and cross-eyed stare behind his thin circular lenses made me feel uneasy. I'd need to keep an eye on him.

After the meet and greet, all of us made our way to the resort's pub. We started out divided by country and then divided again into smaller subgroups. I ended up part of a motley crew of six. We found we'd all extended our stay in Europe several days beyond the official study abroad program, and the group tossed around several potential destinations we could visit together. Venice, Rome, Vienna, and Amsterdam were a few of the target destinations. Kristen, one of the two girls in the group, spoke fluent German—a skill the other five of us couldn't claim—so her inclusion in the group was a monumental victory.

Several beers later, the German and American groups intermingled. "Why do you drink your beer warm?" was the most profound question I could summon under pressure. Thank goodness I had no aspirations of working for the State Department. The Germans informed me their beer wasn't warm but "basement temperature" and they liked it that way because it was of a much higher quality than American beers, which need to be chilled excessively to tolerate. Although I agreed, I felt compelled to defend the carbonated wheat and barley beverages from my home country. Also, let the record show they took the first punch. Friendly ribbing continued throughout the night until Dan interrupted—and not just us but everyone in the pub.

He climbed onto a table to sing the German national anthem while everyone watched with mouths wide open. Halfway through his first stanza, he wobbled and fell onto the tile floor. There were a few gasps, and then several German students rushed over to help him back into his seat. None of them appeared surprised by the incident. That was how my first day in Germany ended.

For the next two days, all of us students attended introductory lessons about our courses. After our group dinners, we huddled together at the resort pub into the early morning. I got to know the other American students in the study abroad program better as we each shared more of our background and told stories. Scott shared his version of his black eye story that involved a perilous descent down a non-existent hill in Central Illinois on his mountain bike. The topic of siblings and birth order came up when Brad blurted out, "I'm a mistake."

The pub went dead silent for several seconds, and then we all erupted in laughter.

"What—what did you say?" I asked as I tried to regain enough oxygen to speak.

Brad smiled and leaned forward. "My brother and sister are in their forties and my parents are in their sixties. My mom was 41 when she had me. I have a nephew that is older than me. My parents didn't think they could get pregnant again, so I was a mistake."

The group howled again, and we discussed Brad's family until we all retreated to our rooms for the evening.

Forty-eight hours after arriving in Germany, I'd yet to see anything outside of the conference rooms, dining hall, or pub. Although I still had four weeks before my return flight, I was growing restless. The session on international currency arbitrage droned on, so I began to doodle. Since Brad's comments from earlier that morning still weighed heavy on my mind, I drew a stick family with a comment bubble coming from the smallest stick saying, "I'm a mistake." Like a class clown in the fifth grade, I took turns flashing it to the others around the room. Scott smiled. Abby let out a small laugh and put her hand over her mouth. Greg stared at it for several seconds, seemingly confused, and finally formed a smile. Brad burst out laughing and couldn't stop. It disrupted the instructor, so I slammed my notebook shut and pretended to pay attention. That was a dead giveaway that I was the guilty party. The instructor's neck turned red, and in broken English he asked me, "Do you have something to share?"

"No, I don't. I won't let it happen again."

He stared at me deep in my eyes and wouldn't look away. I squirmed in my seat, and that seemed to satisfy him because he turned back to the whiteboard to resume the lesson.

The monotony of all the classes and time indoors wasn't my only complaint. I also wasn't thrilled with the food. Growing up in the Midwest on a bland diet of meat, potatoes, and pasta made me a fairly picky eater and leery of anything not in those essential food groups. My preference was something familiar, so one evening I passed on the dinner option I couldn't safely identify. Once hunger pangs kicked in later that evening, I blurted out enough German to the lady on the phone to get a pizza delivered.

On our third day at the resort, we boarded a shuttle after breakfast for our first planned excursion. I was cautiously optimistic I'd get to see the Germany I'd pictured since I booked my flight. Forty-five minutes later, we reached the bank of the Rhine River. The Gothic spires of the Kölner Dom, or Cologne Cathedral, appeared in the windshield and dominated the skyline as we crossed the Hohenzollern Bridge. We parked nearby and, on foot, approached the seven-hundred-and-fifty-year-old structure—the tallest twin-spired church in the world—with proper reverence. I entered the building under the gaze of a half-dozen saints memorialized in granite and paused to let my eyes adjust to the darkness. While waiting, I felt the enormity of the interior by the echoes of footsteps and voices. When I could see again, I stood still and admired the architecture, the statues, the altar adorned in gold, and the stained-glass windows throughout the cathedral. After twenty minutes of walking around the main floor to view monuments and art, I joined the group to climb over five hundred steps to the top of the North Tower observatory, where we could see for miles. I turned in all directions and focused on the mighty Rhine snaking through the city of Cologne. The view washed away the funk I'd been infected with for the last two days.

After leaving the cathedral, the group walked through the shopping district until we found an inviting outdoor café. I selected the one item I recognized on the menu, a bratwurst, and we people-watched for hours until it was time to return to the resort. Before boarding the shuttle, I turned to get one final look at Cologne and smiled. This was indeed the Germany I'd flown over five thousand miles to see.

We had one more day of seminars at the resort, followed by one more evening in the pub with our new

German friends. That final night, Dan attempted an encore performance of his tabletop solo, but before he could get a note out, he fell again and hit his head on the corner of his booth. His head split open, and blood trickled down and around his left ear. A member of the resort staff rushed him to the hospital to get stitches. The German students took it all in stride. I gathered that Dan's antics weren't rare.

After lunch the next day, we said a temporary goodbye to the German students and left for Paderborn. I'd done my research on the city and knew it boasted over one hundred and thirty thousand residents and shared the German industrial state of North Rhine-Westphalia with the notable cities of Dusseldorf, Dortmund, and Cologne. I also knew it dated to the eighth century, when Charlemagne built a palace near the two hundred springs that formed the mouth of the Pader river. Paderborn University hosted over twenty thousand students on its campus just south of the city center. I couldn't wait to see the city and the campus, and to meet the family who would provide my home for the summer.

Chapter 7

The introduction to my host family took place in a banquet room with floor-to-ceiling windows offering a view of the quad at Paderborn University. Professor Carlson tapped me on the shoulder and pointed to a middle-aged man with white hair and glasses and a woman in a floral-patterned knee-length dress and a cardigan. Armed with that tiny bit of information, I nodded to Scott and we crossed the room to them. They smiled as we approached.

"Hallo, wie gehts?" I said ("Hello, how are you?"), exhausting all the German I felt comfortable enough to speak. They replied at length in German and then stared at me. By the looks on their faces, that's when they realized my opening line was the extent of my German-language abilities, so they turned to Scott and smiled.

"Hey, I'm Scott. Nice to meet you."

They looked at each other and responded to Scott in German. He shook his head, and that's when it became clear they knew as much English as Scott and I knew German.

"This is going to be awkward," I whispered.

We all fell into an uncomfortable silence, smiling and pretending to be far more interested in the person serving the shrimp appetizers than we should. The agony ended when Veronika, our hosts' daughter, arrived and introduced herself. Veronika attended Paderborn University and looked to be around my age. She also spoke fluent English with a distinctly British accent. Veronika formally introduced her mother and father, Sue and Karl, and I let my shoulders relax as the awkwardness dissipated. I learned Karl was an engineer at a cabinet factory and Sue was a retired teacher. They'd chosen to take students from America into their home because of Veronika's aspirations to visit the United States in the future. They wanted to help her brush up on her English.

We left the university and put our luggage into Karl's Volvo. Then Scott and I arrived at Veronika's silver hatchback with a manual transmission and a backseat best suited for a small child or large dog. I offered the front seat to Scott, and we followed Karl and Sue toward our new home base for the next four weeks.

"What happened to your eye?" Veronika asked Scott.

"You should see the other guy," I blurted, then broke out in laughter. Scott shot me daggers with his eyes. He preferred to tell a different tale, but my joke still had a solid week of life left before his eyes healed, and I was going to take full advantage of it.

"I fell off my bike," Scott hissed.

Ten minutes later we pulled off the highway, and the vehicle crept through the village of Delbrück. In the town square we passed a church dating back seven hundred years, dozens of local shops, and several restaurants with patrons dining outside. I wanted to jump out and soak up the authentic German experience just outside the car's windows.

Several blocks past the town center, we pulled onto a residential street and then into the driveway of a two-level home. It wasn't the traditional half-timber style home common in ads featuring the central European country. Cream-colored bricks extended from the first story to the second story until they reached the open box gable roof with black tiles. Once Veronika parked in front of the two-car garage, Scott and I grabbed our luggage, and I did a full 360-degree turn to familiarize myself with my new temporary home. Although the house could have been inserted into most suburban US cities and fit right in, the yard was different from any yard I'd seen back home. It burst with colorful flowering shrubs and leafy trees that whispered for me to step under their cool shade and sit in the grass. I could see only the rooftops of the houses on either side even though they were only feet away. It looked as if I could get lost in their backyard, and I secretly hoped it would happen.

Veronika led us inside and up a set of stairs to a loft. It had two beds in one corner, a couple of couches with a coffee table between them, and a full bathroom on the opposite end. We had access to the entire second story of their home. After dropping off our bags, we followed Veronika back downstairs for a tour of the house.

On the first level, she pointed down the dark hallway to all their bedrooms and then opened the door to the family room, where they watched TV together. A few more steps down the hall, she opened the door to the kitchen. All the rooms had doors, and they were all closed. I'd thought it was because they had new visitors in their home, but I later learned this was common in homes in the northwest area of the country.

I examined the stark white kitchen while Veronika showed us the pantry and refrigerator and gave us permission to help ourselves. The refrigerator was less than half the size of the one at my parents' house and only slightly larger than the one in my dorm room. It didn't have a freezer.

"Is that your only refrigerator?" I asked.

"Yes," Veronika replied with a grin.

"It's so much smaller than what I'm used to. Plus, almost all the fridges in the US have freezers."

"We like to have fresh food, so we shop more often. My mom goes grocery shopping almost every day," Veronika explained.

It made sense, but I still believed a full-size fridge with a freezer would be a practical addition to any German kitchen.

"Can I buy some foods I like and store them in your refrigerator?" I asked after my quick scan of the refrigerator revealed only a carton of orange juice, a jar of strawberry jam, and a bag of sliced salami.

"Sure. There's a grocery store only a ten-minute walk away, or we can take you."

While I was mentally building a grocery list, the back door opened and a guy our age entered. He planted a kiss on Veronika's lips, and she introduced us to Arndt, her boyfriend. They'd had been dating for over a year, and he was a regular guest in their home. Fascinated with the unique looking appliances and interesting gadgets, I wanted to explore more, but I also wanted to respect their privacy, so I returned to the loft.

Later that day, we attended a picnic for all the American and German students in the study abroad program and their host families. This time, we rode with Arndt in his silver Opel. Karl and Sue drove separately again. Arndt spoke little English, so our common language was the electronic dance music he played at dangerous decibel levels and his Formula One–driver tendencies. I grasped the door handle until my knuckles turned white every time he shifted his manual transmission Opel into a lower gear to pass another vehicle. In the weeks that followed, Arndt and his Opel made for exhilarating trips to the grocery store. He showed us how Germans overtook slower cars in the center of a two-lane highway. The other drivers, traveling in both directions, drifted into the shoulders to let him pass down the middle. Arndt demonstrated this maneuver at least ten times on our way to the picnic, which was precisely nine times more than I needed to witness. I confirmed Germans hated to be late for anything, even a picnic.

The event was a welcome opportunity to meet my American peers and their host families. Brad, one of our "gang of six," was hosted by a single man in his late twenties named Boris. He proudly wore leather pants and Harley-Davidson T-shirts that prominently displayed the American flag. The lanky man with reddish-blond hair smiled widely as he shared his love for everything about America—along with his hope to visit someday. He seemed more like a big brother who'd buy beer for a group of teenagers waiting outside a liquor store than the host of a foreign exchange student, but that's why we liked him. Boris boosted the gang of six up to the squad of seven when he was present.

The following day, we all met on the University of Paderborn campus for our international business class, led by Professor Carlson. We reviewed case studies of successful German multinational firms, such as Siemens, Henkel, and Volkswagen, and broke for lunch at the central cafeteria on campus. The process to purchase food and beverages was akin to that in a hospital cafeteria or museum in the United States. We selected items from a vast array of choices, then paid at the register.

I chose some kind of pork schnitzel, chips, and a Coke, as did the five other American students. We sat next to some of the German students we recognized at a table connected with others to create one long table. A few minutes into lunch, I looked up and down the table at the dozens of students and noticed nobody else had drinks. I checked out the other tables full of students eating lunch and found the same thing. The Americans and Boris were the only people who had beverages.

"Don't you drink anything with your meals?" I asked Christian, who was sitting next to me.

"No, we are here to eat. We'll drink later," he replied, and continued to crush his meat and veggie stew.

I soon found out what Christian meant. After class ended at two o'clock, all of us students met at the university bar in the center of the quad. The German students were already on beer two or three. They'd saved their deutsche marks for the adult beverages after classes were over.

The discussion started out cordial, but after a few beers, any semblance of politically correct filters vanished on both sides. The German and American students each shared the subtle yet annoying differences we noticed about each other. I believe I heard "superficial," "loud," and "obnoxious" as charges from the German side of the table, while "cold," "pretentious," and "pushy" were volleyed back by the American side. A few rounds later, the German claims had escalated to how they did things better than anyone else in the world. They noted precision manufacturing and engineering, citing famous German brands such as Porsche, Bosch, Montblanc, BMW, Adidas, and Mercedes-Benz as evidence. I'm not sure which brand had cut deep for Brad, but he shouted, "You forgot about starting the World Wars."

Now the gloves were off. The German side returned fire by hurling insults regarding slavery, the Jim Crow laws, and Americans' treatment of Native Americans. Part of me was mortified we'd fallen to the level of competing atrocities, but the other part of me was impressed with the Germans' knowledge of US history. In fact, they were more knowledgeable about our history than most Americans. Then Brad, who had a quick wit and a sharp tongue, went for the jugular.

"Adolf Hitler. Enough said."

The table got quiet for a few seconds, then erupted with more charges from both sides, but I couldn't make out any of them with all the shouting.

During the chaos, I managed to find a moment of levity. Christian slid down in his seat next to me as if hiding from the verbal attack, so I leaned over and asked him, "Do you ever want to move to the United States?"

He straightened and leaned away from me, looking suspicious. "Would you ever live in Germany?"

I thought about it for a second and nodded. "I'd like to try to live in Germany for at least a little while someday. I think I'd enjoy living here. What about you? Do you want to live in the US?"

He shook his head rapidly. "Nein, nein."

"Then why are you going to ISU in the fall?"

"I want to see America and experience your culture, but I don't want to live there. Germany is my home."

I nodded. This was the same response I'd received from the other German students I'd asked during my first week in their country.

I'm embarrassed to admit this now, but before I arrived in Germany, I'd assumed everyone in the world wanted to move to the United States. And by everyone, I mean every single human being, so it shocked me to learn none of the Germans I'd talked to wanted to move to the US. Even Boris had said he didn't want to move there permanently. They all wanted to visit our cities, beaches, monuments, and national parks, and then return home.

Despite the atrocities that had left deep, permanent scars on their land, Germans were content to live in Deutschland. It was their home and they loved it. And this was a sentiment I understood and respected.

Chapter 8

After the lively experience in the university pub, Scott and I returned to our loft in Delbrück to pack for our first trip to see more of Europe. Earlier in the week, the gang of six had discussed using our first rail pass days to visit Vienna and Munich. Vienna wasn't on my original list of target cities, and I knew very little about it. The idea of an extra eight hours on a train for one night in eastern Austria also didn't thrill me, but I didn't want to be left behind.

After Scott and I had dinner with our host family, Arndt drove us to the train station in Paderborn, where we met the other four in our group. We boarded and found an open second-class cabin that fit the entire gang. Unfortunately, our rail passes didn't allow us to occupy a (more comfortable) sleeper car on the overnight train to Austria. Our cabin had seats that pulled out until they were flat, like the bed in my parent's old pop-up camper, and we slept like six hot dogs in a package. I was up most of the night, too wired and uncomfortable to sleep. Hours later, when I finally got tired enough to fall asleep, an Austrian conductor startled me awake asking for our tickets and passports, as we were at the border. His arrival was jarring. He slammed open the sliding door, flipped on the overhead light, and started barking orders in German. This happened every couple of hours after we'd crossed into Austria.

Each time, we'd scramble for our bags. On the advice of another traveler, I'd secured my Army-issued green duffel bag with *Property of the US Army* stenciled on the side to the overhead luggage rack with a lock, which delayed the presentation of my ticket and passport. This annoyed the conductors and stressed out everyone else in the cabin, so I gave up locking my duffel bag after the third intrusion.

We arrived in Vienna fourteen hours after we left Paderborn, and I immediately sensed a buzz in the air. It was a week before the start of the World Cup, and the locals were amped up for their national soccer team. We walked from the train station until we found a hostel near the city center. After we dropped off our bags, we hit the town. Scott studied the guidebook and suggested we visit Sigmund Freud's home. Without looking at a map, Kristen said we should take the route via the Danube River. It sounded like a reasonable suggestion, although it took us nearly a mile out of the way, but we all assumed the longest river in Europe would be a crown jewel of the region. We were wrong. It wasn't horrible. It was just a river running through a big city. So instead of walking along the river to the Freud residence, we took a subway. We walked the final blocks to the address Sigmund Freud called home from 1891 to 1937, when he fled to London because of his Jewish ancestry before World War II.

The Sigmund Freud Museum was closed when we arrived, so we took some pictures of the building and chose another route back to our hostel. As we strode beside pristine gardens, flower beds, and well-maintained courtyards, I was struck by Vienna's cleanliness and manufactured beauty. It was easily the cleanest large city I'd ever visited.

Back at the hostel, exhausted from the lack of sleep on the train and the long walk, we napped. The weather was cool, so we slept with the windows open until the shouts of a large crowd outside woke us. It sounded like a riot. I raced to look out of our fourth-story window overlooking the city center and saw streets full of raucous Austrians. My first reaction was they were angry protestors looking to take out their frustrations on all foreigners, especially Americans. A public display of anger in a European city had to be all about me, right?

Once the fog of my afternoon slumber lifted, I noticed their banners and realized they were soccer fans. Minutes earlier, Austria had lost to Germany, the defending World Cup champions, in a critical match, and the locals were blowing off steam. After the rowdy crowd passed, we returned to the streets of Vienna.

Now that we were fully awake, we aimed for St. Stephen's Cathedral, which towered over the Vienna skyline like two decorated soldiers. From a distance, it looked similar to the Cologne Cathedral—due to the Gothic and Roman architecture the two shared—but their differences grew more evident as we got closer. Unlike the monotone roof of the Kölner Dom, the modern, ornate tile roof of St. Stephen's Cathedral sparkled in the sun, a recent benefit after the original wooden roof burned down and was rebuilt after a fire during World War II.

The six of us climbed to the top to soak in the vistas of the vast city dominated by five- and six-story black-and-red-tile-roofed buildings, interrupted only by a vast array of church steeples. We stayed for nearly an hour to observe all four quadrants of the first major European city we visited that summer. Once we descended from the tower, we found an outdoor café that served both of what had become my go-to items on a German menu—bratwurst and roasted chicken. We ate and watched the locals and the tourists from around the world pass by until it was dark. Then we went back to our hotel for the night and turned in early. We had to catch the eight o'clock train to Munich in the morning.

Leaving Vienna in the light of day allowed me to see the natural beauty of the Austrian countryside. On more than one occasion, I had to close my eyes and shake my head to refocus on the jagged mountains and lush green valleys just outside our cabin window. The landscape didn't look real.

Three hours after leaving Vienna, we arrived in Salzburg, where we changed trains. Unfortunately, we hadn't allowed ourselves enough time to explore the city of *Sound of Music* fame beyond a couple of blocks from the train station—a decision I still regret to this day.

Once the train stopped at the Hauptbahnhof (main train station) in Munich, we quickly found a cheap hotel a few blocks away and then made a beeline for the Marienplatz (city-center square), wanting to make the most of our time. Local street performers lined up to share their craft under the shadows of the towering St. Peter's Church and the four-hundred-year-old Glockenspiel clock with its twice-daily fifteen-minute show featuring life-sized models of men and horses.

We missed the show, so we consoled ourselves inside the famous Hofbräuhaus restaurant and brewery. We'd worked up a thirst traversing Austria, and beers by the liter seemed like the ideal way to hydrate. The Hofbräuhaus delivered on every stereotype a tourist might expect to find in Bavaria: waitstaff in the traditional Bavarian attire of dirndl dresses or lederhosen, heavy glass beer steins, enormous pretzels, and accordion-rich folk music. I was in cheesy tourist heaven and stayed until it closed.

The following day, we took a two-hour train to southern Germany near the border of Switzerland. The famous Castle Neuschwanstein, rumored to be the inspiration for the majestic castle at Disney World, was our destination. We exited the train in Füssen and took a ten-minute bus ride to a parking lot, from which we walked the rest of the way. I looked up as I stepped off the bus and noticed a roof and turret nestled on a hill, a carpet of emerald forest blanketing rugged granite mountains forming the perfect backdrop.

As I strode up the paved path to the nineteenth-century palace, my mouth opened wider with each step. It didn't look real in the pictures, and even in person, it was still hard to believe the beautiful castle nestled in the fog-covered mountains was something I could touch. Once inside, we joined a mandatory tour to explore the living areas and learned King Ludwig II of Bavaria had built the immaculate structure on the hill with his own and other private funds—a Herculean feat at that time. As the rooms with gold-plated walls and copper ceilings started blending together, each window we passed called me outside.

I suggested we check out the mountains outside the castle and they all agreed. At the next exit, my friends and I left the tour and the designated path to climb the side of the mountain that burned itself into my mind the first time I saw an online image of Castle Neuschwanstein. Thirty minutes later, the six of us reached the summit, turned around, and sat to admire the view. Nobody said a word. No questions, no jokes, just silence. It was the proper way to take in the masterpiece God had painted before us.

We returned to Munich late that evening and hit several clubs noted as popular in the guidebooks. Either we'd arrived on the wrong night or the guidebook writers weren't much fun—we chose to go home early rather than keep striking out at boring clubs with twenty-dollar cover charges.

I woke the next day to rain pelting the single-pane glass windows of our hotel. It slowed to a drizzle as we donned our ponchos and boarded the local train headed to the town of Dachau. Once we arrived, we walked several blocks to the Dachau Concentration Camp Memorial at the former forced labor camp ten miles outside Munich. It was the first Nazi concentration camp when it opened in 1933, and hundreds of thousands of prisoners spent time at Dachau during the twelve years it was operational.

The gang of six split up so we could walk through the rooms at our own paces. I stared at the pictures of the prisoners and studied the pain and despair on their faces. The lump in my throat grew as I observed the piles of shoes, teeth, and strands of hair that belonged to the men, women, and children in the pictures hung throughout the facility. After I passed through the brick incinerator room, I was ready to leave. I found the others and told them I'd wait outside, but they also wanted to go.

My mind ached from trying to comprehend the scale of the atrocities committed on the grounds. I followed the gang through the neighborhoods outside the death camp toward the train station as if drunk on confusion. I looked up at the homes and silently judged everyone who had lived in the area and done nothing for the twelve years Dachau operated at the edge of their neighborhood. But then I felt sympathy for those who'd wanted to do something but felt helpless or afraid they'd end up on the other side of the menacing wall.

During my time in Germany, I was hard on the Germans for the evil that transpired in their country, but I must also give them credit where it is due. Today, they face the Holocaust head-on. The events of the Holocaust are part of the mandatory curriculum for all German students. Elementary school students regularly visit former concentration camps on field trips. No doubt they leave shaken and a bit scarred from them, much as I did, but also committed not to let anything similar happen on their watch.

Once we reached the train station, I wanted nothing more than to go back to my loft in Delbrück. The others agreed, so we packed up and sprung for the ICE high-speed train, which would get us back to Paderborn several hours sooner.

Today, I can still see the pictures of the skeletal-looking humans pictured throughout Dachau. They're burned forever in my memory.

Chapter 9

The day after Dachau, I slogged into the classroom on five hours of sleep, still barely functioning after three cups of coffee. The German students immediately marched over and started peppering Scott and me with questions about juice and a white bronco.

I was confused. There wasn't a TV in my host family's loft, and I hadn't watched a minute of news since I arrived. I assumed they were mixing up their English, or they'd even started drinking early because nothing they said made any sense to me. It wasn't until later that day that I caught the news of the O.J. Simpson low-speed chase on BBC News, which Karl watched during dinner. The O.J. Simpson saga was big news in Germany, and the Germans I knew talked about it all summer. They all shared their love for American pop culture, especially our movies and music, but I sensed they also enjoyed our drama.

Professor Carlson resumed the lesson on international business we'd begun the previous week, and after the class was over, he dismissed the German students and asked the Americans to stay behind for a few minutes. Once all the Germans were gone, Professor Carlson leaned against the desk.

"I know you didn't come all the way to Germany to sit in a classroom," he said, before straightening and walking closer to us. We were eager to hear where this was going.

"This will be our last class on campus. You need to attend the events and field trips on the itinerary, but that's it. No more classroom instruction. We'll touch base again when we get back to the United States."

The original schedule had called for two classes three days a week as part of our study abroad program, and I'd paid tuition for six credit hours for our time in Germany. I wondered if I'd still get them all. This wasn't my only worry. Everyone in the room was excited to hear we had more free time, as we'd have exponentially more travel opportunities, but I didn't have enough money to travel for an additional two weeks.

As the six of us walked through the quad and discussed what this additional free time meant, everyone agreed it would be criminal not to take advantage of this opportunity. I had to express my concern, though. "I want to see as much as possible while we're over here, but I didn't bring enough money to visit all these countries we've talked about."

"Didn't you bring your ATM card?" Greg, another guy in our gang, asked.

I nodded. "The card isn't the problem. It's the pittance I have available in the bank when I use it."

Two others shared that money was a concern for them as well, so the gang debated how to travel economically. Most of our transportation was prepaid, making lodging, food, and beverages our most significant travel expenses. After some discussion, we all committed to pinching our pennies and making the additional travel possible by sharing rooms and buying food in grocery stores instead of restaurants.

As soon as I got back to my loft in Delbrück, I called home and begged my mom to send me a gift pack of "normal food" as soon as possible. I'd considered making this call sooner, but now it was a necessity.

My mom had been great about sending me weekly packages of treats and newspaper clippings while I was in basic training, so I figured this would be right up her alley. The only difference was that overnight express to Germany would cost more to ship. A lot more.

"Can't I just ship it regular mail?" she asked.

"No. I asked around, and that will take at least two or three weeks. Maybe longer. I'll be gone by the time it arrives."

The line went silent, so I knew I had to up the stakes. "I've already lost ten pounds in less than two weeks."

"That's good," Mom replied.

"No, that's not good!" I yelled into the phone. "I'm losing weight because I don't like any of the food over here." Which was true, although I was mostly afraid to try anything new.

"We'll see if I can get something together."

As any parent or child knows, "we'll see" is usually code for "I won't do it, and I don't want to talk about it anymore." I needed a commitment.

"I had to eat horse tongue last week," I said.

This was also true. While in Munich, I'd ordered a mysterious item off the menu at the Hofbräuhaus. I'd finally agreed to divert from my safe diet of bratwurst and roasted chicken at the behest of two Austrians sitting at our table. It looked like Spam, so I took one cautious bite, chewed, and swallowed it. The Austrian couple belly-laughed when they saw my nose wrinkle.

I slammed down the fork. "That's disgusting!"

They continued howling when they told me I'd just eaten horse tongue, but I wasn't laughing. I was out fifteen deutsche marks with a hideous taste in my mouth, semi-nauseous, and still hungry. I'd almost called home asking for "real" food that night.

"Fine," my mom said. "I'll get some groceries tomorrow and send out the box in the afternoon."

"Thanks, Mom. You're the best!"

Scott made the same call, and his mom agreed with less of a fight. We were on our way to securing much-needed comfort foods from home and significant savings on food. Beverages were the easiest to save money on because beer was always the cheapest item on the menu. Many restaurants didn't offer tap water, and beer was less expensive than soft drinks, milk, juices, and bottled waters, which were mainly carbonated mineral waters. Choosing to drink beer to save money was yet another sacrifice I had to make to see more of Europe.

We'd all agreed to stay in hostels to save money. Hostels were popular with backpackers and budget travelers in Europe because they offered the essentials—a bed, a roof, and a locking door—at a deep discount compared to traditional hotels. They had community bathrooms and showers, and the better properties also offered a breakfast of pastries and watered-down coffee. It was common to find a hostel in a major European city in an excellent location for forty to fifty US dollars per night.

Despite these cost-saving measures, we wouldn't have the time or money to properly see all the cities on the wish list of six people. So we decided we'd spend just a single night in all of them to experience a sliver of the culture in these great European cities. It was like hitting all the sample trays in a club store on a Saturday—we wouldn't get the full experience, but we'd get a taste of everything.

We had two days of field trips to banks, museums, and the local chamber of commerce in Paderborn, and then we'd take our first bonus trip. The first such trip was to Amsterdam.

The clang of the train bell echoed throughout Amsterdam Central Station as we arrived in the Venice of the North. We secured our overnight bags and burst out of the train station and into a bustling city center in the early afternoon. The streets and sidewalks were wide to accommodate the trams, cars, and scores of pedestrians. Several blocks in, we turned and walked until we hit our first canal. We followed the narrow street along the canal and passed inviting hotels, shops, and restaurants. Leafy trees growing along the canals broke up the parallel-parked cars and sea of bikes parked in racks. Bikes and bikers were everywhere. Today, nearly sixty percent of residents ride their bikes daily on the four hundred and fifty miles of bike paths in Amsterdam.

I'd been expecting seedy streets and rundown buildings because I'd only heard about Amsterdam's red-light district, known for its debauchery. Instead, I passed smiling pedestrians and restaurants with cheerful-looking diners enjoying their meals under colorful canopies and beside public art.

After finding a hostel that could accommodate the guys in one room and the ladies in another, we set out to find the red-light district. At first, we passed it without even realizing it. It looked like every other thoroughfare in Amsterdam, with shops overlooking the narrow street, parallel-parked cars, and canals running down the middle. The only indications we were in the right spot were the red lights on the decorative concrete bollards at the end of each block. Once we arrived, it took a little time to work up the courage to walk through the corridor.

Curiosity finally won over, and we meandered through. I was underwhelmed and shocked at the normalcy inside the boundaries of the infamous district. There were several shops whose names were displayed over banners of red, green, and yellow stripes or cannabis-leaf logos coming out of coffee cups, which I'd expected. Then we turned the corner, and my jaw almost hit the pavement.

Women and men dressed as women gyrated behind three-by-eight-foot plate-glass windows like movable mannequins. A few ladies of the night waved at the six of us, and we teased each other about who they were targeting. I still say it was Brad, since his cheeks were the reddest. The gang gasped collectively when a woman dressed in lingerie that matched her red lipstick opened her glass window and helped a young man inside. They moved behind a curtain together after she pulled a cord to illuminate a red light. I witnessed live the reason for the district's name.

After the sun set, we hit a few clubs in the area, but most were dead midweek, so we walked up and down the canals and watched the eclectic crowd enjoying the balmy weather. The next day we tried to visit the Heineken brewery for a tour, but it didn't open until after our train back to Germany departed. There was so much more I wanted to do, including visiting the Rembrandt House Museum and the Anne Frank House, but we didn't have the time. We left Amsterdam less than twenty-four hours after we arrived in order to be back in Paderborn in time for our class trip to Berlin. I vowed to return someday to enjoy more of what Amsterdam offered.

Chapter 10

The sun was just peeking over the horizon when I stepped onto the bus and found a seat for the five-hour trip from Paderborn to Berlin. Once we arrived in the formerly divided city with nearly four million residents, the bus driver turned tour guide drove through wide streets with grand medians brimming with lush trees. The streets resembled those of newer cities in the US, such as Dallas and Charlotte. The driver explained that because so much of Berlin was bombed to rubble during World War II, the Americans helped rebuild many of the streets based on the designs they were most familiar with. After the tour, we checked into a hotel, which was paid for by my study abroad fees. A private room with my own bathroom and a TV, it was the nicest I'd stayed in up to that point.

That evening the opera at the Berlin State Opera House was on our itinerary. I'd never been to the opera before and was eager to attend a culturally rich event. Once the performance began, I tried to pretend to understand or care about what the woman was singing passionately about in Italian but just couldn't. The others in my group felt the same.

Together we concluded Professor Carlson only said we had to attend the opera, not stay until the end, so based on that technicality, we ditched the opera at the first intermission and found a beer garden next to Tiergarten Park. This enormous urban park full of trees, gardens, ponds, and playgrounds lay in the middle of Berlin. Think Central Park in Manhattan. We found an open table large enough to accommodate the six of us, ordered beers, and watched the locals enjoying their time in the ideal weather. My back sank into the cushioned chair, and I didn't move for hours. People-watching in the park was the perfect activity after the whirlwind of grueling travel.

The next day we boarded a new bus for the guided tour I'd been waiting for since I first saw it on our schedule months earlier. Ever since the Berlin Wall came down and I watched people dance, hug, and kiss in the square under the Brandenburg Gate, I'd wanted to see the infamous wall and plaza for myself.

First, the tour guide took us to the Berlin Zoo, the most visited zoo in Europe, and then the Olympic Stadium, home to the 1972 Olympic Games. Next, we passed through the former heavily fortified Checkpoint Charlie—the best-known Berlin Wall crossing point between the Soviet-held East Berlin and the Allied-controlled West Berlin during the Cold War. I got out to snap pictures of the signs in English, French, German, and Russian warning citizens of the danger of crossing. Plaques contained stories of brave East Berliners who snuck into West Berlin hidden in trucks or cars. I tried to imagine the angst they must have felt as they approached this checkpoint during the Cold War. It had a tower with snipers and floodlights surrounded by razor wire and concrete barricades. If that weren't bad enough, you were sure to encounter combative Soviet soldiers with snarling German shepherds hungry for defector flesh. My stomach turned at the thought of any attempt to cross such a dangerous zone.

I didn't need the tour guide to tell me what our next stop was. I immediately recognized the neoclassical monument and backdrop of the 1989 protests. The Brandenburg Gate, with its six pillars supporting the Quadriga—a statue of the Roman goddess of victory in a chariot pulled by four horses—was one of the few surviving structures in the area after World War II. It served as a functional gate for pedestrians and vehicles moving from the Soviet sector in East Germany to the British sector in West Berlin until they completed the Berlin Wall in August 1961.

The bus pulled up to a curb, and everyone exited onto Pariser Platz, the large pedestrian square east of Brandenburg Gate. In 1994, several sections of the Berlin Wall were still intact, so I left the group and walked to a portion of it. It bore graffiti regarding the fight for freedom years earlier. I closed my eyes and revisited images in my head of people dancing between the swings of the sledgehammers taking down the oppressive wall. The wall still had stories to tell, and I could feel each one as I ran my fingers across it like a needle across a record player. I don't think "The Wall," by Pink Floyd, was actually playing on loudspeakers when they tore down the Berlin Wall, but it came to mind every time I remembered the historic event. The

Brandenburg Gate was the first area to be breached in 1989, allowing East Germans to flee the communist USSR into West Germany.

After spending ten minutes along the wall, I boarded the bus early and sat quietly by myself. I'd seen what had inspired me to study German culture and attempt to learn the language. I peered out the window at dozens of cranes in the former East Berlin, rebuilding what had been lost to neglect and decay under communism. I'd just stood where freedom won over oppression. This experience alone had been worth the trip.

The second leg of our tour took us to Potsdam, in former East Germany. It was here the Potsdam Conference among the three Allied powers of the United Kingdom, Soviet Union, and the United States occurred in July 1945 to devise the post-war plan for Germany after their unconditional surrender. Everything looked and felt different from the former West Berlin a few miles to the east. The buildings were varying shades of gray, and their facades were cracked and crumbling. Chunks of concrete rested on the sidewalks below. Many still had the scars of machine-gun bullets as a stark reminder of what had taken place on that same street fifty years earlier.

New information on the history of the area that has shaped generations since the end of World War II came at me fast, and I soaked it up like a sponge. Learning isn't just interesting or fun for me: I crave it like oxygen. This might make me a little weird—okay, a lot weird—but I'd rather go on vacation to a place with historical relevance than a sandy beach. Of course I enjoy spending a little time at the beach, but I get restless just sitting under an umbrella sipping fruity drinks with their own umbrellas. Now, if that beach is near a historic site or city to explore and investigate, I'm all in. Sign me up.

I've always preferred to trample on the same cobblestones or climb the same stone fortresses as people who lived hundreds and thousands of years before me. Knowing that humans resided in cities without modern plumbing, electricity, cars, and smartphones yet led functional lives inspires me. As different as their living conditions were back then, they had wants, needs, desires, and emotions similar to ours today. They wanted neighbors with whom they could share a common cause, friends with whom they could experience the joy of breaking bread, leaders they could trust to support the community, and lovers with whom they could grow old. My heart beats faster every time I turn a corner and witness ancient structures with storied histories or local people living life in town squares radiating their culture and customs. Learning is my drug—specifically, learning about historic people and places. That's a major reason I'm pulled toward Europe.

That said, as much as I love learning, taking in large quantities of new information can also be taxing. Being in Berlin, I soon felt as though I'd just finished an eight-hour-per-day training seminar held over several days. Physically and mentally exhausted after the tours, I suggested to the group that we find a place to eat and park ourselves there for the night. They agreed, and we stumbled upon a raucous Irish pub near our hotel.

Every TV was showing a World Cup soccer match. We arranged enough tables and chairs for all of us to sit together, and for three hours, I ate, drank, and watched a game that was making more sense to me each time I did so. Since I had no team to root for, I'd made it a personal rule to cheer for the team represented by the country where I was currently staying. Germany wasn't playing, so I decided to cheer for Ireland since we were in an Irish pub instead of the Netherlands national soccer team. This was a wise move. The local Irishmen in the pub adopted our gang of six into their group of rowdy fans, and we all cheered Ireland to a surprise victory.

I felt lighter when I left the pub. The weeks of struggling with foreign languages, being lost, and not getting enough sleep had taken their toll. The Irish pub provided the mental recharge I needed. Not trying to understand German or speak German. I just talked and cheered in English without thinking, and it felt amazing. Now I understood why the Germans always asked if I spoke German and appreciated even my feeble attempts to speak their first language.

For the first time during my trip, I felt a little homesick. A part of me wished I was back home in the USA. I swelled with empathy for anyone who visited the United States with a limited grasp of English. Traveling in a foreign country can be hard enough, but it's exponentially more challenging when you can't speak the local language. My appreciation for transportation-hub signage, restaurant menus, and ATMs that feature multiple languages is immense.

Chapter 11

"I hope we have something waiting for us at the loft," Scott said as the bus entered the Paderborn city limits.

I eagerly nodded my agreement. I was more than ready for some of my favorite foods.

Veronika picked us up, and as soon as we got back to our host family's place in Delbrück, Scott and I dashed up the stairs and found that we each had a brown box on our bed.

"They made it!" I shouted.

It was like Christmas morning. Tearing into mine, I found boxes of Kraft Macaroni & Cheese, Lucky Charms, Pop-Tarts, and a large pouch of beef jerky—a shelf-stable, highly processed smorgasbord of comfort foods to ensure I wouldn't wither away. I dumped my goodies onto a table next to the jar of peanut butter and loaf of bread Scott's parents had sent to him, then hurried down to the kitchen to prepare a gourmet lunch of mac and cheese for Scott and me. We had to eat fast because our train to Paris departed from Paderborn in two hours.

Our original plan had been to go directly from the bus station to the train station across the street after returning from Berlin, as the other four in our gang of six had done, but on the way, Scott and I decided we wanted to collect our goodies and stock up for our next trip. After we packed peanut butter sandwiches and Pop-Tarts into our backpacks, Veronika took us back to the train station. I'm still grateful today for the patience and hospitality of Veronika and her parents during our stay in Germany.

In the early evening, we arrived at the bustling Gare du Nord (train station) in the center of Paris. We wanted to explore Paris as soon as possible, so we found an affordable hostel with three rooms available in the 11th arrondissement and dropped off our bags. We strolled up and down several streets and ended up near the opera house in Bastille Plaza.

It was dinnertime, and we were fortunate enough to find a table at an outdoor café within the shadow of the July Column. We ate and watched Parisians and tourists enjoy the historic square. Then the bill arrived and ruined our mood. None of us had converted the French francs listed on the menu to US dollars before ordering, and the prices were far higher than we'd assumed. The real kicker was the charge for the ambiance. It turned out the privilege of eating in Bastille Plaza had its own charge. I spent half of the francs I'd exchanged in the train station at my first stop in Paris.

We headed back to our hotel under the golden glow of the sunset. It was near the summer solstice, so the sun continued to cast its light over Paris well past ten o'clock. Despite the light, we turned in to stock up on sleep for a long day ahead of us.

The following day, we left the hostel after devouring the homemade pastries in the tiny breakfast nook on the first floor. Then we power-walked thirty minutes to the Père-Lachaise Cemetery to see Jim Morrison's tomb. This hadn't been my first choice on the list of possible activities, but it was free and a few of our gang were big fans of the former lead singer of the Doors, so I went along with the group. I was glad I did. Drifting through the 110-acre property with towering memorials and chiseled granite monuments allowed me to absorb recognizable names like author Richard Wright, playwright Oscar Wilde, and composer Frederic Chopin, among many other names I did not recognize that were responsible for the rich history of the region.

Once we left the most visited cemetery in the world, we sprung for subway tickets to cover the five-mile journey to the Eiffel Tower. When it was our turn, we crammed inside the elevator to ascend to the observation deck at the top. Seconds after the lift doors opened, the City of Lights revealed her awe-inspiring views. I moved to the edge and analyzed the layers of the city, which reminded me of growth rings on a tree. From where I stood, I could see the fountains in the Trocadéro gardens below my feet, the Arc de Triomphe a little farther away, and modern skyscrapers in the distance. Next, I moved to another side and treated myself to handsome views of the Seine River, bustling with commercial and pleasure boats passing under bridges crowded with pedestrians. *Is there a more perfect place for a romantic cruise than the Seine?* I asked myself.

I took so many pictures I had to replace my roll of film before I moved to another side. There, I was struck by the well-manicured Champ-de-Mars green space extending southeast for blocks. I stared with envy at the ant-like people covering nearly every patch of grass until I spotted an open corner. That cool strip of green called to me like the mythical Siren song—I just had to go. I shared my idea to have lunch on the grass with the gang of six, and they hustled to the elevator with me.

We purchased cheese, crackers, and cheap wine from a shop below the Eiffel Tower and found my targeted patch of grass. Each of us lay directly on the turf to absorb the warm sun. I watched wispy clouds scatter across the indigo sky while listening to the laughter of our neighbors in the park. I've never felt more Parisian than at that moment, but we couldn't stay. We still had more Paris to see.

We walked over one of the bridges I'd seen from the Eiffel Tower and soon entered the gigantic horseshoe-shaped plaza in which the Louvre Museum was located. The plaza contained three small glass pyramids and one central pyramid larger than the other three combined. A rectangular reflection pool with a couple of fountains surrounded the main pyramid, calling crowds of people to rest on its black granite ledge. We'd just walked a reasonable distance on a warm day, so we joined them. That's when the "ugly" American in our group revealed himself.

Brad decided he needed more immersion in the local culture, literally, so he took off his shoes, pulled up his Levi's, and waded back and forth across the black marble pool in front of one of the most distinguished museums in the world. I was expecting a wave of angry French men and women to drive us out of town, but nobody said anything as Brad frolicked in the hallowed waters of the Louvre and the rest of us laughed. I did observe several eyes rolling and a general disdain for his actions, but no one made a peep. The stereotype of the French being rude was ruined for me at that moment. In fact, the French were mainly friendly to me during my brief stay.

Once I finally stopped laughing so hard my stomach hurt, we helped Brad clean up so we could go inside. As soon as we'd paid our admission, we bolted into the prestigious museum as though a bell had gone off to start a horse race. A few study abroad students we met in line from Connecticut told us a few popular exhibits get very crowded so they are best to hit first. Our destination? The *Mona Lisa*. I don't want to ruin it for anyone who hasn't seen the famous Leonardo da Vinci painting in person, but if you have seen it, you'll understand when I say that it wasn't what I expected. We took our illegal pictures (with the flash off, of course—we're not heathens) and then slowed our pace to see the other exhibits. The French crown jewels and the Egyptian ruins were two that caused me to stick around and admire a little longer. The stories of the generations of people behind the relics were just as impressive as the items behind the glass.

After the Louvre, we walked to the Notre-Dame de Paris and meandered inside the sacred halls of the medieval Catholic cathedral. We didn't have the energy to climb more stairs, so we decided to rest outside in the Square Jean XXIII Plaza, where we found open benches under trees near the ivy-lined walls along the Seine. The peaceful garden atmosphere allowed us to recharge before our red-eye train ride back to our host families in Germany.

We arrived back at Gard du Nord exhausted from walking all day. We spotted a local bar nearby, and since we had some time before the midnight train left, we headed inside. We were already wary of the high prices when the bartender asked if we planned to sit or stand. "Sit," we replied in unison, and he informed us the price was double if we sat at the bar or a table. We quickly changed our answer and took our bottles of Kronenbourg 1664 to an open area and sat down. The tile floor was hard, so we put all our backpacks in a pile and huddled together as if we were in a rescue raft escaping our capsized ship. Six tired and foul-smelling American students intertwined on a pile of packs in the middle of the bar caused more than one potential patron to enter and then quickly leave. Then I pulled out a box of Lucky Charms, and we took turns sticking our hands in to grab a handful of dinner. I'm pretty sure I saw smoke pouring from the bartender's ears.

I'm not familiar with profanity in French, so I didn't know what the bartender said, but his disgust was obvious when he motioned wildly for us to sit at the bar.

"Hurry up and sit before you scare away more patrons," he said in English with a thick French accent before he wiped his hands and threw his towel in our direction.

"And put that box of . . . of charms away!"

Chapter 12

The overnight train from Paris arrived in Paderborn just after sunrise. Scott and I took a bus to Delbrück and slept most of the day, then went to Brad's house to watch another World Cup soccer match. Germany was playing, so Boris, the host, had invited twenty or so friends over and set up a wonderful spread of homemade dishes, potluck style, on picnic tables in his backyard. Not wanting to offend anyone, Scott and I tried all the new dishes. I didn't like most of them and neither did Scott, but finally we tasted something that surprised us.

"This is actually really good," I said to Scott.

"I know," Scott replied, and took another bite. He then turned to the German guests and held the food on his plate high for everyone to see. "That's some good scheisse," Scott said, using the German word for "shit." "What is it?"

A German guy stood and shouted, "That is not scheisse!"

Scott and I burst out laughing, but the German guy was genuinely offended, so Scott tried to explain. "I know. I like it. It's delicious."

"Then why did you call it scheisse?"

A crowd formed around us, so I backed away to give Scott plenty of space to explain himself.

"Um, uh, in America, that's a compliment."

The German's face softened a bit. "I don't understand."

Scott looked like a deer in the headlights as he stammered to explain English slang. Thankfully, another German saved him. "It's like the eff word in English. It's used for everything. Right?"

"Yeah, kind of like that," Scott said with a look of relief on his face.

The offended German smiled. "I am going to the United States in the fall. I don't know how to use the eff word like you do in America. Will you teach me how to use the eff word properly?"

Scott nodded and grinned like a proud father. "You can use it as a noun, a verb, an adjective . . ."

An eyewitness to the beauty of diplomacy in action, I swelled with pride and then went inside to watch the match. Germany was playing Bolivia. I'd invited Veronika and Arndt to join the party. Arndt was a big soccer fan, and I hadn't spent as much time with Veronika and him as I'd initially hoped, so I figured this would be an excellent opportunity to get to know them better. Arndt explained basic soccer strategy that was still foreign to me throughout the match and together we helped cheer the German football team to a 1–0 victory over the Bolivians. It was growing apparent I was a good luck charm for whatever soccer club I adopted for the game.

The next day, Veronika took Scott and me to a nearby swimming hole. The lake was only the size of about two football fields and surrounded by spongy green grass that tickled my bare feet. It was the warmest day in Germany since we'd arrived, so locals covered almost every inch of turf with towels and blankets. Kids and mothers waded in the shallows. The water was too cold for me, so I leaned back on my elbows and soaked up the sun. When I closed my eyes, I heard laughing and splashing and could easily imagine this swimming hole was one I often visited in Illinois. That conclusion vanished when a young mom claimed a spot next to us and put down a blanket with her three children in tow. She slathered sunscreen on her kids, who looked to be between the ages of four and seven, and then took off her bikini top. I felt my jaw opening and quickly slammed it back shut. Nobody else seemed to notice or care. I didn't want to be the creepy American, so I looked away as if I'd just stared directly into the sun. Despite the regularity of women removing their tops while sunbathing throughout Europe, it startled me every time I saw it.

That evening, Scott met up with some other friends while Veronica, Arndt, and I went out for drinks. We didn't stay out long and returned home to play cards in the loft. I taught them a new game, and they proceeded to beat me at it every time. As we played, I took the opportunity to ask a few questions about German culture.

"How do you say 'excuse me'?" I asked.

"Why do you want to say that?" Veronica replied.

I should have expected her next response, given that she'd answered my question with a question, but I persisted. "I like to say 'excuse me' before I push through people to get off a crowded subway or bus. Usually, people in Germany don't say anything. They just push through."

Veronika and Arndt looked at each other and laughed. "We don't need to say anything. If we need to get to a place, we just go there, and maybe we push a little to do it."

"Yeah, I guess, but I don't want to be rude."

"It is not rude to us. Germans understand your intent and just move."

Despite her explanation, this didn't resonate with me. I was from the Midwest, where we apologized if we passed someone walking too slowly in the grocery aisle or reached in front of someone to snatch our favorite salad dressing off the shelf. The avoidance of rude behavior, or even the perception of it, was part of my culture, and not saying "excuse me" wasn't okay with me, but I let it go for the moment.

After Veronika and Arndt tired of beating me at cards and retired to their room downstairs, I stared at the ceiling for an hour trying to process the idea of not saying "excuse me" before pushing past people. Finally, I resigned myself to just saying "excuse me" in English for my benefit—and sanity.

At this point in my European travels, various cultural differences I'd once found interesting and even endearing frustrated me. I'd initially hoped to fit in like a natural-born European, so I wanted to love everything about every country and culture, but of course, I couldn't. Not putting ice in drinks, pushing by people without saying "excuse me," mixing beer with soft drinks, eating lunch meats for breakfast, using deodorant conservatively—these petty "offenses" were getting on my nerves. I knew it was partially because I was mentally and physically exhausted from the lack of sleep, poor diet, and brutal travel schedule, but it was more than that. I missed the comforts of home. I wanted to be me without having to think about saying or doing the right thing. I wanted my culture, my food, and my customs.

The next morning, I rose at the same time as the sun to board a bus for the final scheduled event of the study abroad program. Our last destination was the Rhine River, the second-longest river in Western and Central Europe. I'd been looking forward to this date on our itinerary since I admired the impressive river from the top of the cathedral in Cologne during my first week in Germany. Approximately seven hundred and fifty miles long, the Rhine River starts in Switzerland and flows north through Germany and the Netherlands until it empties in the North Sea. It's a popular route for river cruises, and our study abroad group of Germans and Americans would experience a short tour.

First, we made a pit stop at a winery called Burg Eltz, just south of Cologne. We explored the cellar carved deep into the mountainside and took part in wine tastings before ten o'clock in the morning. The complimentary Rieslings and other white wines went down smoother than expected, and I sported a wine-induced grin as we boarded the specialized vessel to navigate the rivers of Europe. It was about twenty-five feet wide but only one story higher than the deck to accommodate the ancient bridges built across the river.

Once our ship cast off, I positioned myself in the sun on the top deck to better view the majestic stone fortresses—some that dated back two millennia to the Roman Empire—lurking around every bend and watching over the waterway like sentinels. When it was time for lunch, I headed below deck and watched villages and vineyards pass my window between bites of my sandwich. Several hours and dozens of castles later, we docked in Koblenz at the confluence of the Rhine and Moselle rivers.

After exploring the mid-sized German city, we marched up a nearby hill to a hostel in a former fortress overlooking the city. In my assigned room, I cleaned up for the farewell dinner. Two hours later, I arrived in the ballroom with two long tables at the other end of the fortress. The German and American students were instructed to mingle, so I took a seat between two Germans I'd gotten to know during my three weeks in the country. A member of the local chamber of commerce welcomed us to their community, and then they served dinner. Roasted chicken was an option, so I was delighted. During dessert, the student advisors from each country—Professor Carlson and table-dancing Dan—took turns sharing the program's highlights and thanked everyone in the room.

Afterward, I had the urge to be alone. The end of the study abroad program was near, and I wanted to soak in the final moments without distractions or conversations. I left the ballroom and sauntered along a paved trail to the property's highest point and leaned over the concrete railing to see for miles in all directions. Melancholy washed over me, and I imagined the former Roman, Frank, and Prussian soldiers and citizens standing in the same position centuries earlier while watching the river turn orange and the hills blacken, their silhouettes kissing the golden sky in the setting sun. It felt fitting to be viewing this sunset, as the sun was also setting on the study abroad program. My time with the German students I'd grown to admire and respect was over.

Although I was bummed my time in Europe was near its end, I was also looking forward to returning to the United States. I'd loved every place I'd visited, but none of them was home.

The following day, the other American students and Professor Carlson left Koblenz for the Frankfurt airport, ninety minutes east. That would have been too easy for the gang of six. We were on our own time now and still had more countries to visit. We weren't done yet.

Chapter 13

A month after I landed in Frankfurt, my mind was jammed full of memories I'll never forget, and I still had another week before my return flight home. Those experiences wouldn't have been possible without strict adherence to a tight travel budget, but this also came with a cost. I walked over two hundred and fifty thousand steps to save money on transportation. Taxis weren't an option, and even bus and subway fares added up, but walking was always free.

Sleeping was also a problem. I don't sleep well—or at all really—when I travel, so the red-eye trains to save money on lodging meant hours of listening to the rhythmic thumping of the tracks below me while the rest of the gang slept in the cramped cabin. I was grateful for the abundant availability of coffee from my fellow coffee lovers in Europe. The gift box of comfort foods from home provided a nice boost, but eating what I could afford on a shoestring budget wasn't a recipe for a wholesome diet. In short, I was exhausted.

The end of the study abroad program coincided with the high point of my frustration as a budget traveler in foreign lands. It was a slow build, but weeks of irritation with language barriers, questionable food options, and minor cultural differences eventually boiled over. I yearned for the comforts of my culture, but the thirst to drink up all the niceties of Europe was still strong. I couldn't wait to get home, but I also didn't want to ever leave.

A primary source of frustration was the frequent travel by buses and trains. Outside of a few trips as a passenger in Veronika's or Arndt's cars, I never enjoyed the luxury of a personal vehicle. I don't know whether "you snooze, you lose" was coined in Europe, but it certainly applied to every form of public transportation in my experience. There was no lollygagging to your seat unless you wanted to stand for ten hours from Berlin to Paris. Whenever the doors of a bus, train, or subway opened, it was a mad dash to find a seat.

I learned this nugget of European culture early, so it didn't directly affect me too much. I was pretty nimble boarding trains and buses, and so were most of the others in our gang of six. But Greg had two speeds, no matter the circumstance: slow and slower. I lost count of the times we raced to get a six-person cabin on a train or six seats together on a bus only to have Greg arrive late and lose his seat. Saving an open seat without a butt about to land in it wasn't an acceptable practice in my experience across Europe. When we'd say "That seat is taken," the response from the person who'd sat down in the saved seat was always the same. They would look around, say, "I don't see anyone," cross their arms, put on their Sony Walkman headphones, and act as if we didn't exist.

We didn't want to leave Greg behind or see him stand for hours, so we often took turns standing or even switching to a different train that took longer because it was less crowded. My frustration was forty percent a result of the impatient Europeans and sixty percent a result of Greg. Five of us learned to adapt to this nuance of European travel, but he never did, and that screwed us all over on an almost-daily basis.

I was self-aware enough to know that in the final days of my trip, my exhaustion was getting the best of me, and I risked ruining my remaining days in Europe and perhaps even my memory of the entire trip. I was letting every rude remark, every menu not printed with English, and every push in the back to move me out of the way get under my skin. The abundant cultural similarities seemed invisible and quiet, while the occasional cultural differences felt enormous and seemed to scream in my face. I couldn't maintain the status quo if I was going to enjoy the rest of my time in Europe. I needed a change. And so, I took the lead.

With a few "must-haves" still on my wish list, I coordinated the gang's next trip. This expedition would differ from the others we'd taken so far, at least for me.

Having watched other tourists with envy as they ordered something other than processed pork sausage links or spaghetti while also enjoying a soft drink with their meal, I chose to tap into my emergency savings account. I needed a few more comforts and conveniences that traveling on a strict budget didn't allow.

I called my bank and moved five hundred dollars out of my emergency savings account and into my checking account so I could access it at an ATM in our next country. Then, over coffee in Koblenz the next morning, I sold my idea to spend a little more on our next trip and end our time in Europe on a high note to the rest of the gang. Either I was a better salesperson than I'd given myself credit for, or money wasn't as tight for the other five, but they all agreed, and we set our plans.

The next day I would wake up in the number one city on my Europe wish list. We were going to Rome, Italy!

Chapter 14

The six of us had sprung for an upgrade to a sleeping cabin for the fourteen-hour ride to Rome, and despite a sleeping area slightly larger than a coffin, it was a slice of heaven compared to our previous overnight trips.

When I woke shortly after sunrise, we were in the heart of Switzerland. I rubbed my eyes to be sure I was fully awake and the scenery outside was real and not just a dream. The steep, snowcapped mountains and rolling emerald valleys below looked like a painting that never ended. The stunning natural beauty continued around every bend and beyond every tunnel. I pressed my nose against the window for hours watching the Swiss countryside unfurl outside the train. As we descended, the sharp mountains transformed to hills and slowly gave way to plains as we approached Rome.

In the Eternal City, the gang of six secured two hotel rooms near the Spanish Steps, and then we made a beeline for two of Rome's greatest attractions. We explored the site of the nearly three-thousand-year-old Roman Forum first, then visited the iconic Colosseum. The latter was high on my wish list, so we hurried to catch the last tour of the day. The staff whisked us through, and I could only quickly observe and snap a few photos of the arena that once seated over fifty thousand people. For me, the four-story stone and concrete Colosseum in Rome is the physical embodiment of ancient civilizations. Each seat, wall, and arch had a story to tell, both good and bad, and I wanted time to sit and listen for those whispers from the past. I didn't want to just visit the Colosseum; I wanted to experience it. However, the tour staff kept us moving through each stop quickly, so I left disappointed.

As the sun lowered in the western sky, I found myself ravenous for authentic Italian food. Near our hotel, we found a restaurant still mostly empty around 7:00 p.m., and the six of us sat down to enjoy our first five-course meal in Italy. The antipasti (appetizer) was followed by insalat (salad). Then came the primi (first course), which in Italy typically doesn't include the main protein, followed by the secondi (second course)—the main meat or seafood dish. Finally, we topped the meal off with dolce (dessert) and a shot of grappa to help us digest the three thousand calories we'd each consumed. I leaned back in my chair and let the dopamine course through my veins until I got the bill. My portion was 30,000 lira. Heat shot up my back as I considered that one meal in Rome might have drained my entire life savings.

"What's the conversion rate here?" I asked in a panic.

"Fifteen hundred lira to one US dollar," Abby, the other female in our group, said.

I quickly did the math. The best meal I'd had on the Continent so far was only twenty dollars. It tasted even better after I learned it was affordable.

We wobbled out of the restaurant just as it got busy around nine and found a spot on the Spanish Steps to continue digesting our feast. The grand stairway, composed of 135 steps, rises from the Piazza di Spagna, one of the most popular plazas in Rome, to the Trinità dei Monti church. Dozens of people sat on the steps eating, drinking, and talking on that beautiful evening. The energy was infectious.

While we relaxed, Kristen shared she'd kept in touch with an Italian exchange student she'd befriended in high school who lived in the suburbs of Rome. She floated the idea of calling Luciana to see if she could meet us and show us around. We loved the idea and encouraged Kristen to contact her friend.

The next morning, Kristen made the call and Luciana insisted we all come to her home for lunch. I was all in for a home-cooked meal, so we boarded a train and forty-five minutes later, Luciana's mother greeted us beside a long table on their outdoor patio. It was flanked by their beautiful two-story home, which was painted gold with white trim. A wall of Italian cypress trees soared forty feet into the sky behind the house. I was a bit shocked and envious by the size of their home. It looked similar to some of the homes behind gates and long driveways outside Miami, Florida, yet humble enough for an upper middle-class Italian family. We took our seats, and this time we enjoyed a five-course meal for lunch—and a homemade one at that!

The entire meal took three hours—two hours for lunch and one hour for multiple grappa shots. I didn't have to worry about digestion problems, or walking for that matter. We took the train straight back to our hotel and napped until 9:00 p.m. Now I know why the siesta is still practiced in Italy.

We met Luciana again, for dinner at a pizzeria, and this time she brought friends with her: a young couple and Claudia, her single friend. When I first saw Claudia, I knew I'd met my future wife. She was as beautiful as a movie star and returned my shy smile when I shook her hand.

"Hello," I said.

She smiled back. And that's when I noticed a potential problem in my wedding plans. Claudia spoke as much English as I spoke Italian—zilch to be exact. How was she going to know how charming and funny I was? Our relationship was doomed from the start, and the breakup happened so fast I don't think she even realized what was happening. At any rate, she took it well.

Attempting to recover from the pain of lost love, I joined everyone at the table in the middle of the crowded pizzeria. After I'd crushed the most fantastic margherita pizza ever, the music started, and several patrons jumped on stage—it was karaoke night. After an hour of Italian songs with indecipherable lyrics but catchy beats, someone sang a song in English. Seemingly inspired, Brad leaped to his feet and went to talk to the DJ. He returned with a sinister grin.

"What did you say?" I asked.

"I told the DJ we were in a band from Chicago and want to sing a song for our new Italian friends."

"What? Did he believe it?"

"I don't know if he believed it, but we're next," Brad said, then turned to the DJ as the music faded.

He pushed Scott, Greg, and me toward the stage, and we each grabbed a microphone. The audience of locals clapped and cheered after the DJ introduced "a band from Chicago," and I turned to face the monitor. Thankfully, familiar lyrics popped up, and the four of us proceeded to sing the worst rendition of the Righteous Brothers' "You've Lost that Lovin' Feelin'" in the history of humankind. Despite our best attempts to summon our inner Maverick and Goose—*Top Gun*, of course—the crowd started booing us at about the halfway point. Still, we soldiered on. I didn't dare make eye contact with anyone on my way back to our table, and then we all burst out laughing at our pitiful performance.

We left the bar well after midnight, and Luciana's friends, who were a couple, left for home. I assumed that was the end of our long and eventful day, but Luciana had no intentions of going home so early, so the eight of us stood outside the pizzeria talking. I shared my disappointment regarding our quick tour of the Colosseum.

"Follow me," Luciana said, as she waved for us to catch up. Ten minutes later, we were back outside the Colosseum, its arched entrances blocked by thick iron gates at least eight feet high.

Someone stated the obvious. "It's closed. We can't get in."

"Watch this," Luciana said, and slipped her slender body through the gate. Claudia did the same, while the rest of us stood with our mouths open in disbelief.

"Come on, try it!" Luciana yelled. Greg and Abby made it through, but two five-course meals and fear of needing to call the Roman fire department to free a "stupid university student from America" prevented my passage.

The rest of us walked around the perimeter and found we could scale the gate if we targeted the section closest to the wall. Minutes later, everyone was up and over, and we passed through several arches to the seating area used to observe gladiators battling beasts for their life.

Under the light of the moon, we sat in silence and scanned the maze of caverns snaking under the former arena floor, now twenty centuries old. The wooden planks covering the caverns had rotted away, so I had to imagine the surface that hosted the epic battles. I squinted a little and tried to imagine what it must have been like to sit in the arena and cheer for a favorite gladiator. Luciana and Claudia whispered to each other in Italian, and I imagined the Roman emperors and citizens who'd sat as spectators in my exact spot. It felt surreal to have the whole place to ourselves.

I felt the gravity of where I was and what had occurred two thousand years before me. Many individuals perished in this spot, often in a barbaric fashion, and that wasn't lost on me. My admiration is for the structure, not the activities that transpired inside, because when I was younger, I thought people who lived thousands, even hundreds of years ago were mostly primitive. All the good stuff had come from people born after 1900, I figured. I couldn't have been more wrong. Ancient cultures had accomplished so much with much less in terms of information, tools, and technology. My respect for those engineers, builders and people of that era has since skyrocketed to the moon.

I eventually laid back on the stone slab to gaze at the same stars as the ancients, but soon after I did, Luciana grabbed my arm and whispered, "Get up and follow me."

I sat up and saw the beam of a flashlight moving below us. It was a security guard. I'd been so immersed in the experience, I'd forgotten we were trespassing. I followed Luciana as she roused the others. She led us down a corridor and stairs on the opposite end of the Colosseum as the security guard. I jogged behind her, my chest pounding with fear and excitement. At the gate, Kristen, Scott, Brad, and I climbed over while the others slipped through.

A block away, we exchanged high fives and congratulated each other on our dramatic escape.

"I have one more place to show you," Luciana said.

Continuing our string of trespassing offenses, we followed Claudia and Luciana down into the Forum, the former plaza of the ancient city. This time we stayed closer to our escape route, and I leaned against three-thousand-year-old pillars, not daring to lie down again. Sixty minutes later, the blue hour arrived, foreshadowing the sunrise that would soon follow. We left before anyone noticed us and said "ciao" to Luciana and Claudia. We arrived back at our hotel after the sun started filling the streets and the rest of Rome woke up.

After a few hours of sleep, we walked to the Vatican and saw Pope John Paul II speaking to a large crowd. The Pope spoke in Italian, so I couldn't understand his exact words, but I could feel them. Next, we toured

Saint Peter's Basilica, and I drifted past the gilded walls and smooth marble statues without saying a word throughout the holy structure. After that we hiked to the other side of the Holy See to take in the Sistine Chapel.

And then it was time to bid farewell to four members of the gang of six, who were heading to Frankfurt to catch their flights back to the United States. It was a bittersweet departure. I was grateful for their company during my time in Europe, and I looked forward to seeing them again, but traveling in a group of six is far more challenging. I wanted the last few days before my departure back to Chicago to be as simple as possible. Scott and I walked them to the train station and after hugs, handshakes, and promises to meet up again on the campus of Illinois State University in the fall, they disappeared into the crowd.

And then there were two.

My next mission was to consume more delicious Italian food. At the Fontana di Trevi, Scott and I purchased paninis from a street vendor and ate them on the Spanish Steps. Our last night in Rome wasn't high on the adventure scale, but thanks to Luciana and Claudia, my travel mojo was back, and I was ready for our next destination.

Chapter 15

The cabin went pitch-black for twenty seconds and then filled with bright sunlight. Again and again. I pictured a slow-motion strobe light as our train passed over bridges and through tunnels in Northwest Italy. Nice, on the French Riviera, was our capstone destination, and we intended to relax.

After a quick stop at the Italian seaside villages of Cinque Terre, three Americans joined Scott and me in our cabin. They had attempted to travel into France the day before and told us the French were embroiled in a train strike that affected all trains in the French Riviera and we'd have to disembark and take a bus or taxi to Nice once we hit the border. They were now making their way back to Genoa after a wine tasting in Cinque Terre.

This was awful news. We'd have to add hours to our trip, plus waste precious funds on alternative transportation for the final twenty miles to Nice from the border.

"Do you still want to go?" I asked Scott.

"Nah. Sounds like a big hassle."

I suggested heading back to Paderborn early. "We could catch a train in Genoa."

Scott shook his head. "I was hoping to relax on the beach."

We were both quiet through a few tunnels, and then I broke the silence. "I have an idea."

Scott straightened in his seat and looked at me eagerly.

"Let's do something spontaneous."

I floated the idea of getting off at a random stop somewhere in Italy and spending a couple of nights there—no planning or reading guidebooks on places to go or things to do. Just pop off the train and pray we'd find a place to stay.

"Planned spontaneity" might be an oxymoron, but it felt right as our train passed the numerous seaside communities of the Italian Riviera overlooking the sparkling azure waters of the Mediterranean. I didn't think we could go wrong. Scott agreed.

Peering out the window, we analyzed each new seaside village with the careful eye of a future visitor. At each stop, Scott would ask "Is this it?" and we'd both stick our heads out the window.

"Nah, let's keep going" was my response every time. Nothing felt like the right place yet.

Genoa, a large city, was fast approaching—we had to decide soon. Finally, we arrived at a stop that looked like all the others, but at this particular station, a man was leaning up against his red Ferrari.

"That's a sign," I said. "Let's get off here."

We pulled our backpacks off the train and watched our transportation leave, brimming with anticipation.

Then I looked up at the signage and learned the name of our new home for the next two nights: Santa Margherita Ligure, Italy. We soon learned it was a small town of fewer than ten thousand residents located twenty-two miles southeast of Genoa in the Liguria region.

I took a moment to inhale the salty air before following Scott down a steep, narrow street into the charming seaside community. We trekked until we found an affordable hotel a few blocks away from the main harbor—the town was shaped like a hand, with the harbor and central plazas in the palm and the hillside homes nestled in the fingers. It was one of the nicer hotels I stayed at during my time in Europe, complete with a private bathroom and a beautiful view of the sea if we stood on the bed and looked over the rooftops outside our window.

It was late June, and the weather was warm, so we changed into shorts and walked until we found a sliver of open beach. After a couple of hours of sunbathing we were ready for dinner, so we walked to the plaza in the center of town. Once we arrived at Liberty Plaza near the statue of Santa Margherita, we found a pizzeria playing a World Cup game on a large TV. A small crowd was gathered around it, primarily American tourists. Scott and I joined them and cheered on Italy as they battled Norway.

During the game, I officially ruined any calzone experience I'd have in America for the rest of my life. That pizzeria served the world's best calzone—a turnover made with pizza dough and filled with prosciutto and cheese. I also munched on breadsticks and drank Peroni beer as the crowd grew. More local fans kept arriving, and the multinational crowd cheered on the Italian players as they held off the favored Norwegians. When Italy won, all the Americans jumped up and hugged each other as if we'd been fans of the Italian national team since birth. I'd noticed this kind of obnoxious behavior wasn't appreciated in every country, but Italy wasn't one of them. Here, it was encouraged. The locals were so impressed with our passion for Team Italy they joined our group of tables and bought several rounds of drinks and appetizers. Even with all the excitement of the night, the highlight was the calzone. I might have even dreamed about it. I vowed to return for another one in the future.

After lunch the next day, Scott and I took a trolley to a beach a couple of miles outside Santa Margherita. The water of the tiny lagoon was so clear you could see the rocky bottom twenty feet down. The heat drove us to leave our stake on the shore after a few hours, so we caught the trolley again and disembarked near the main harbor. I noticed people walking down the hills from the homes perched high above the harbor. They were coming from all directions. Curious to see where they were heading, I scanned the area and noticed dozens of small boats arriving in the harbor. I followed the crowd to a pop-up fish market, where the ships offloaded their catch into bins—red fish, white fish, octopus, clams, and a dozen other varieties of seafood. A white-haired woman with a handwoven basket snapped up a couple of fish and an octopus and handed them to the fisherman so he could weigh and wrap the fresh catch in paper. Seconds later, she was on her way back up the hill. My love for this village swelled. I imagined this scene had been playing out for hundreds and maybe even thousands of years on these same shores.

The next day, it was time to leave our Italian home. I packed slowly and meandered up the hill back to the train station. I wasn't in a hurry to leave Santa Margherita. We caught the next train to Genoa and then to Milan, where we explored the area around the train station until our next train departed. Scott and I had chosen Zürich, Switzerland, as our final destination before returning to Paderborn. The journey through Switzerland was just as beautiful as I'd remembered, but Zürich felt out of place in the picture-perfect scenery. It was clean and modern but felt sterile—and it was insanely expensive for two college students. A plate of spaghetti with red sauce was the cheapest item we could find, and after doing the currency translation, we realized it was twenty-five US dollars. Even with my emergency funds and new positive attitude, I couldn't justify the expense. Days earlier, I'd enjoyed a five-course feast in Rome, and I couldn't help but compare that to the pittance available to me in Zürich for more money.

I felt the negativity I'd shaken a week earlier bubbling up again as we studied every menu posted outside of restaurants. The cheapest hostels were more expensive than any hotel we'd stayed at during our time in Europe. After skimming the tenth menu for something reasonably priced, I wondered if I should just bite the bullet and spend the rest of my savings on a hotel and dinner so I could enjoy my last night in Zürich. Then I remembered passing a McDonald's in the train station.

"You want to head back to Paderborn early?"

Scott turned from the menu and started walking toward the train station. After a few steps, he yelled over his shoulder, "Yeah, let's go."

It might have been a double Quarter Pounder with fries and a soft drink, I don't recall exactly, but I do remember that McDonald's Value Meal was more satisfying than any other I'd had in my life. I don't eat at McDonald's often in the US, but those golden arches can be like a welcome beacon of light to a wayward ship when you're in a foreign country and food options are scary or scarce. Love them or hate them, you always know what you'll get at any McDonald's around the world, and for that, I tip my hat to them.

We purchased our tickets to Paderborn and then leaned against a wall, propped up by our packs for hours until our train arrived, just before midnight. I didn't even care that it wasn't a sleeping car. On principle alone, I didn't want to spend a penny more in Switzerland. That would show them.

Twelve hours later, we were back in northwest Germany. It was a Sunday, and the buses weren't running to Delbrück. Because we didn't want to bug Veronika, our only option was to take a taxi. We crawled inside a tan Mercedes-Benz sedan, the standard vehicle for taxis in Germany, and soon learned the driver didn't speak English. So, it was up to me to give him directions to our loft in Delbrück. I moved to the middle of the back seat, cleared my throat, and began spouting directions in two- and three-word phrases in German. The driver nodded and started driving—in the right direction!

For the next ten minutes, I guided our taxi driver to the driveway of our host family. I told him the street names and whether to turn right or left. It was the most German I'd spoken the entire trip—and by far the most any resident of Germany I'd spoken to understood. On a high, I floated into the house to spend our last night with Karl, Sue, Veronika, and Arndt. We picked cherries from a tree in their backyard, enjoyed dinner together, and played cards until we were too tired to keep our eyes open. On my last full day in Germany, I felt as if I were part of their family. The ideal ending to a great trip.

Early the following day, Karl, Sue, and Veronika woke up early to see Scott and me off. I thanked them and gave Veronika a hug. They'd been more accommodating than I could have wished. I felt tears forming knowing I'd probably never see this generous and kind family again, but I fought them back. Most of them.

A station wagon pulled into the driveway. Dan, the German adviser of falling off tables drunk fame, had arrived to take us to the Frankfurt Airport. Inside the vehicle, I sniffed the air to detect if there was any alcohol on his breath before we entered the high-speed autobahn. Much to my relief, I didn't smell any.

At the Lufthansa Airlines gate, I smiled at the sight of "Chicago" flashing on the departure board. My European adventure was almost over, but I'd soon get to enjoy my favorite comfort foods and speak English to anyone who would listen. I was ten hours away from sleeping in my bed, and I was ready.

Chapter 16

Thirty-five days. Eight hundred and forty hours on the European Continent. And I felt every one of them. In that time, I visited six countries and nine major cities in Europe, most of them in the last three weeks of my trip. I'm still grateful for every person I met and every country I visited. Vienna, Amsterdam, and Santa Margherita hadn't even been on my radar as possible destinations when I left Chicago, and I'd ended up loving all three. The list of things I'd learned and experienced during my time in Europe was long and comprehensive and became forever etched as fond memories in my mind. Despite the challenges, annoyances, and sleep-deprived days, if you asked me a hundred times if I'd do it all over again, I'd say yes all one hundred times.

Once I arrived back at my parents' house, I slept on and off for days to get my circadian rhythms back on schedule. My jet lag was severe, but seventy-two hours after I returned home, I felt normal again. I started eating my favorite foods, watching my favorite TV shows, and hanging out with my old friends. It was great seeing my friends again, but the food was a bit anti-climactic. I think I built up the greatness of my hometown cuisine in my head a bit too much when I was frustrated with the food options in Germany.

The post study abroad meeting at ISU was in early July, and I made the one-hour drive down to the campus to complete my coursework. The entire gang of six was together again, and before class started, we all shared hilarious stories still fresh from our recent trip, and I laughed until my side hurt. I cherished those stories that only they'd understand. Professor Carlson kicked off the class by informing us our study abroad grade would be based on a term paper about our experience in Germany.

The exact topic I chose escapes me, but it was general enough that I could complete it in a week with little research and mail it to Professor Carlson. He wasn't a strict professor—as evidenced by him setting a dozen college students free in a foreign land—but he was incredibly kind when it came to my grades. I received an A on the term paper and a 4.0 GPA for the six credit hours of the summer semester, so my concerns back in Germany were needless. I wished I could have taken part in a study abroad program every summer.

Once I had a dozen rolls of film developed, I carefully organized the printed pictures in a portable photo album in chronological order. If anyone stopped near me or even looked in my direction while the photo album was in my possession, they'd find themselves on the receiving end of my detailed explanation of my epic summer vacation in Europe. I think my mom was the only one who stayed through the entire presentation.

As the days turned to weeks after my return home, I often thought about my experience overseas. Most of the minor annoyances that had frustrated me, like a burr in my shoe, felt distant, while the positive experiences with people and places remained fresh. It was a complete flip. I missed Europe and longed to be back in the tiny hostel rooms with shared bathrooms, back in the public plazas that felt alive. My sentiment toward Europe had grown from casual interest to deep appreciation, and I vowed to go back smarter and better prepared, especially regarding finances. I'd had memorable experiences while watching every deutsche mark, Austrian shilling, and French franc, but it was far more stressful and exhausting doing this than dipping into my savings. I promised myself I'd save up for a larger travel budget for future international trips. I'd learned to navigate some of the differences and nuances of the countries I'd visited, and I felt this knowledge, combined with a larger budget, would allow me to take advantage of everything that made Europe special.

I hoped to get a high-paying job after I graduated. And I also started to consider another idea—what if I got a job in Germany? Would that be the best of both worlds? I'd heard of American university students getting hired by German firms. Was that an option for me?

In August, I moved in with new roommates excited to start my senior year. During my first week back in classes, I landed a job waiting tables at a chain restaurant known for its generous portions of affordable steak. While waiting tables one day during the lunch rush, I started taking the order of four men in suits speaking English with an accent, which I soon recognized as

German. They worked for a global business supply and equipment company based in Stuttgart and were in town for work.

Their accent brought back a flood of memories, and I told them I'd recently returned from Germany. They seemed excited, and I even shared what little German I was comfortable speaking. They offered genuine smiles in return for my attempt to speak their language. I shared that I wished to return to Germany again soon, and that I'd maybe even like to live there.

"What do you want to do?" one of the businessmen asked.

"I'm getting my degree in marketing, so something in that field."

The man nodded at a colleague. "Klaus here is in the marketing department, so maybe he will give you his card so you can share your résumé."

I couldn't believe my luck. "I would really appreciate that."

Klaus handed over his card, and I noted he was a vice-president. He was in a good position to genuinely help me. "Email me your CV," he said, "and I'll share it with the appropriate people."

"Would your company hire an American with a degree in marketing who doesn't know how to speak fluent German yet?" I asked.

"If you are willing to learn German, we will hire you. Are you willing to learn?"

"Yes. Ja." I nodded emphatically to ensure he'd understand my response in any language.

"Then, if you are qualified, we would hire you," Klaus stated, and he turned back to his steak.

Those four men received the best service I could provide. This was the opportunity I'd been looking for.

I emailed Klaus my résumé a week later. For months after I hit send, I dreamed about starting my career at the company's home office in Stuttgart and spent hours researching the city and its history in case I received an offer or simply a phone call. But I also spent countless hours wondering if I'd really take a job in Germany if I received an offer. Would I be willing to start my career in a foreign country where I didn't know a single person?

This was the first time I had to consider the real possibility of living abroad. It was no longer just a hypothetical question. I weighed all the pros and cons. Leaving friends, family, and a culture I was familiar with were cons at the top of my list while the timing was perfect to experience life as an overseas expat. After thinking long and hard about it, I decided I would move to Germany for a job if given the opportunity. I wasn't sure if I was ready to commit long-term, but I figured that, at a minimum, it would be an excellent springboard to bigger and better things on either side of the pond.

I never did hear back from the business supply company, but the seed had been planted. Finding a job in a major European city was no longer just an interesting idea: it was now a high-priority goal. I was determined to set myself up to achieve it.

The next semester I was able to take several electives and chose courses in international finance, international business, and world geography. International finance was more challenging than I expected, but I enjoyed the courses and did well in all three of them.

In May, I graduated, moved into another apartment with one roommate, and joined thousands of recent graduates looking for their first real job. I consulted Professor Carlson before he departed for the summer about my desire to find a position in Germany or anywhere in Europe. He advised me to target large multinational companies since they have employees around the globe and are used to hiring workers from the international talent pool. I created a list of all the multinational companies with offices in Central Europe and began sending résumés to open positions. Months passed without a response, and so, needing to pay my rent, I applied for positions with American companies. Finally, five months after I graduated from ISU, I landed my first "real" job, with a large food manufacturer and distributor—not in the Netherlands, Germany, or Austria but in Deerfield, Illinois, in the northern suburbs of Chicago.

Fortunately, I had friends in the area, so I moved from my apartment near the ISU campus to a couch at a friend's place thirty miles from my office in Deerfield. For six months, I paid rent to store my clothes in a coat closet and sleep on a couch. Finally, I'd saved up enough to afford my own apartment in the suburbs of Chicago.

A year after I started the job, my six-year enlistment in the National Guard was up. I considered reenlisting for another six years but in the end, I knew I wanted to be traveling extensively for work and pleasure and would need maximum flexibility, so I took the honorable discharge.

Several months later, I received a promotion to supervisor. It felt great to have my hard work at the company be noticed, and I wanted to continue to ascend the ranks, so I started taking night classes for an MBA. Although it wasn't Europe, Chicago was fun, and I had a respectable income to enjoy it with. My friends and I hit the restaurants, clubs, sporting venues, and neighborhood festivals in the summer. Eventually, I'd all but forgotten about Europe.

One night over the Labor Day weekend, I met up with friends at a backyard barbeque. Scott moved back home for his job in the southern suburbs of Chicago, so he was also at the party. As they usually did when Scott and I got together, our European travels came up in the conversation. Two years had passed by this point, and we shared our favorite worn-out stories and expressed how much we wished to return. At one point, Oktoberfest in Munich came up in the discussion.

"We should all go to Oktoberfest this year," I said. "Another spontaneous adventure like Santa Margherita." I waited for a laugh or at least a smile.

"Are you serious?" Scott asked.

I wasn't sure. Before I had time to give it much consideration, my thoughts were interrupted. "I'm in," said Jim, our mutual friend. "I've always wanted to go to Oktoberfest."

Now it was my turn to ask, "Are you serious?"

"Yeah," he replied in a sincere tone. "I've been to Mardi Gras a few times and always thought Oktoberfest would be cool."

Scott and I looked at each other and then both turned to Jim, who was now grinning. "I'm serious, guys. Let's do it."

Could I really be heading back to Germany in less than thirty days? The positive feelings I had about visiting and potentially moving to Germany over the past two years began bubbling to the surface. I practically jogged back to my car in the parking lot. After putting on my seat belt, I adjusted the rear-view mirror and noticed the wide smile on my face.

Was this really happening?

Chapter 17

As soon as I got back to my apartment that night, I fired up my AOL account. I'd volunteered to research the events and flights—to no one's surprise—and get back to Scott and Jim. I typed "Oktoberfest 1996 dates" into the search engine.

"What?" I yelled into the empty room as the results appeared before me.

That year, Oktoberfest started on September 21 and ended on October 6. Silly me. Based on the name, I'd assumed Oktoberfest actually took place during the month of October. This was more like Septemberfest—and attending would be a colossal challenge. We had less than four weeks to get to Germany. I assumed the airfare from Chicago to Munich on such short notice would surely kill the deal, but I was surprised to find tickets were affordable.

Even still, I questioned if going on such short notice was possible or prudent. When I called Jim and Scott the next day, I shared my findings and suggested we get a head start on planning for Oktoberfest the following year. They disagreed—my friends couldn't believe our luck.

"Round trip airfare below five hundred dollars per person? That's unheard of!" Scott said.

Plus, they thought it would be fun to be spontaneous about the rest of the travel plans. They were game to book the flight and worry about everything else later. "Just like Santa Margherita, remember?" Scott asked.

I considered their wild plan for a few hours. Part of me was afraid to commit to something on such short notice without time to properly plan. But I couldn't deny the airfare was affordable, and I'd be able to do Germany and potentially other European destinations right this time because we all had decent jobs. After a dinner of cold cereal, I decided I was willing to take a leap—a trip of planned spontaneity. I called Scott back first, then Jim. We booked our plane tickets that day. My worry faded and turned to elation. I was going back to Germany!

Twenty-six days later, we arrived in Munich on a direct flight from Chicago. Since we'd booked nothing in advance, securing a hotel was the first thing we had to do for our week's stay in Munich.

The search didn't start well. We'd grossly underestimated the availability of reasonably priced hotels in Munich during Oktoberfest. Nothing was available. I envisioned the three of us huddled together on a park bench overnight. Our last chance was the local tourism office. The line was fifteen people deep when we arrived. I was already regretting our reckless spontaneity, and I didn't feel much better once we reached the counter. The kind lady with a thick accent found three rooms for us, but they weren't together. We'd each bunk in different hostels with strangers.

"I guess it won't be too bad," I muttered to myself. It was better than the park bench that had been looking like a real possibility.

After receiving our keys, we left to find our sleeping quarters for the night, which were several blocks away. My room had four empty bunk beds. I appeared to be the first to arrive and chose the bottom bunk of the bed farthest from the door, pushed my backpack underneath the bed, changed into a warmer shirt, and met Jim and Scott in the Hauptbahnhof. We took the subway to the official Oktoberfest grounds.

We arrived around ten-thirty that night, and the place was a zoo. All the giant beer tents were over capacity, and the lines to get in were long. We also didn't know all the tents closed at eleven o'clock. The clubs and bars in Chicago stayed open until two or three in the morning, and I'd assumed that was the case everywhere in the world.

As we discussed our next move outside the tents, they closed, and we watched people leaving. Almost everyone was yelling or singing. Many had arms around intoxicated friends to help them walk, and a few immediately threw up on the pavement. The tsunami of obnoxious drunkenness was overwhelming, so the three of us returned to our hostels.

In bed, I put on my headphones, clicked play to start my *Europe Trip Mix* cassette tape in my Walkman, and then slept—until a gaggle of drunk men singing at the top of their lungs in the hallway woke me up.

"Please don't come in here," I whispered.

My wish was not granted. After fumbling with their key for a full minute, the singing men burst through the door. Lights switched on, and the chaos moved into our two-hundred-square-foot room.

They didn't notice me at first. I opened my eyes for a few seconds and saw seven German men about my age stripped down to their tighty-whities singing and dancing at the end of the bunk beds. I couldn't understand anything they were saying, but I could tell when one of them realized I was in the room. He stalked toward me like a leopard waiting for the right time to pounce on its prey.

I panicked and squeezed my eyes shut. Not knowing what else to do, I played dead.

Seconds later, I felt him poke me. Then another arrived and shook me. The singing stopped, and I could feel (and smell) the drunken breath of several men. They seemed harmless and may have just wanted to expand their boy band to eight people, but I wasn't exactly sure what plans they had for me. I knew I had no plans to join their party, so I refused to open my eyes and let them know I was awake. A minute or two later, they left and resumed singing, but it felt like they stood over me for an hour. They must have thought I was either the deepest sleeper on the Continent or dead. I didn't open my eyes again until the sun was up the following day.

During breakfast, I shared my traumatic brush with death with Scott and Jim. They laughed and taunted me with their good fortune—Scott had two quiet and courteous roommates, and Jim's roommates never came home. After taking a sip of coffee, Jim said he didn't want to arrive too late to the Oktoberfest grounds this time and suggested we go right after they opened at 10:00 a.m. First, though, we needed to find a better place to stay, so we tried a few more hotels near the Hauptbahnhof and struck gold, landing a vacant room with three beds. It was in the same hotel I'd stayed at during my visit to Munich two years earlier, but I'd missed it when we passed by the first night because it was under construction. The maze of scaffolding in front of the building must have confused other potential guests. Lucky for us! We paid, dropped off our luggage, and headed for the subway. At a little after ten in the morning, we strutted onto the grounds.

Less than fifty people were in a tent that held thousands, but the mood was still festive. People from all over the world would soon fill the rows of picnic tables in the tent large enough to cover a football field. The Hofbräuhaus was the most famous Oktoberfest tent, so it attracted the most international visitors. As the day passed, we met people from Sweden, New York City, Australia, Denmark, and Ireland. The Irish were the most fun, so we stuck with them for the rest of the day. Incredibly, I didn't notice any obnoxious drunks that night.

Despite what we'd seen the first night, my overall first impression of Oktoberfest was positive. I enjoyed the food, music, beer, and jovial atmosphere. At one point, I stood on top of our table and sang John Denver's "Take Me Home, Country Roads" with thousands of people from around the world, many of whom spoke little English. Chills shot up my back and arms when the DJ cut the music and let two thousand international revelers sing a cappella. The realization that thousands of people from so many countries, backgrounds, and beliefs could be united through a song I grew up hearing on my parents' record player stirred my emotions. I still get chills today when I hear the first few chords of that song.

This turned out to be the highlight of Oktoberfest for me. We didn't visit any of the parks, museums, or clubs in Munich. We didn't even go to any of the other dozen beer tents on the Oktoberfest grounds. Instead, every day, we got up, brushed our teeth, and headed for the Hofbräuhaus tent, where we stayed until it closed. It was as though I were in the German version of *Groundhog Day*.

Finally, after four days, I voiced my concerns over our rotisserie chickens for lunch. "Can we do something else?"

Scott and Jim sat on the other side of the picnic table and stared at me with looks of confusion. "Why?" Scott asked.

"I didn't fly all the way over here to hang out at the Hofbräuhaus the entire time. Let's do something different."

Neither of them wanted to change the routine. They were having too much fun with the status quo, so we went to the same place at the same time and ate the same rotisserie chicken for lunch and again for dinner. It wasn't torture, but I was feeling as though I was letting a rare opportunity to see more of Europe slip through my fingers.

The only break in our routine came in the form of an intruder into our third-story room well after midnight one night. The hotel didn't allow unpaid guests past the front desk, so one young lad was gentlemanly enough to sneak his date up the scaffolding and through our open window.

Scott woke up as the guy was helping his date down from the window frame. "What the eff are you doing?" he yelled.

That woke Jim and me, and I watched in shock as the young couple scrambled for the door. They swung it open just as we got out of bed and gave chase. They turned into the stairwell and lost us a few seconds later. We had to laugh.

Later that day, I left the Oktoberfest grounds early and went back to the hotel. I put in my mixtape and thought about how disappointed I'd be in myself if I did nothing else on this trip. I'd been interested in Prague since my last trip to Europe, and it was a reasonable distance from Munich. I'd been asking other travelers about their favorite stops in Europe, and many listed places I'd been, such as Rome, Amsterdam, and Paris, but Prague was also frequently on the list of top destinations, and it was now on my mental wish list of places I wanted to visit. I fell asleep pondering whether I'd go there alone if Scott and Jim didn't want to go.

After breakfast the next day, I concluded since we had only three nights remaining, I'd visit Prague with or without them. I hoped they'd want to go with me because I found traveling much better when sharing it with friends—especially if those friends appreciated it as much as you did. For me, sharing the experience with someone else is half the fun of visiting new places.

And so, after I finished my scone, I shared my desire to visit Prague. Scott and Jim thought about it for about ten seconds, then said they preferred to stay. It wasn't the decision I wanted to hear, but I remained committed to going by myself. On the way to Oktoberfest that morning, I purchased a ticket for the red-eye train that night, and we all went back to the Hofbräuhaus for lunch. Yeah, more chicken!

After my dinner of—you guessed it—chicken, it was time for me to leave to catch the overnight train to Prague. I was going for only one night, so I told them I'd meet them back on the grounds the night before we left.

I walked away slowly and turned around several times to see if they'd change their mind. Thirty minutes later, I was back at the hotel, where I grabbed my overnight bag. I was going to Prague alone.

Chapter 18

It was like a scene straight out of a romantic comedy. As I made my way to the waiting train destined for Prague, I heard yelling and looked behind me to see Scott and Jim jogging through the station. Jim waved. "Wait for us! We want to go too."

A jolt of energy shot through my body. It wasn't as romantic, say, as a scene where a woman misinterprets her new boyfriend's hug with his older sister who came home early from college and then darts to the airport to fly back to her small town in Montana—she doesn't leave, though, and her dreamy boyfriend catches up and explains everything just before she hands her paper ticket to the gate attendant, who stands and watches the rekindling of their love. Regardless, I was thrilled they were coming. I'd flown across the Atlantic to enjoy Europe with my friends, after all.

They explained they'd made it back to the hotel in time to buy tickets and board the overnight train minutes before it left the station. Fortunately, it was mid-week and Oktoberfest wasn't over for several more days, so the outbound train was less than half-full and Jim and Scott were able to get the same sleeper car as me for the ten-hour train ride. After the train left Munich, I crawled into my tight quarters and managed to sleep for a few hours.

Early in the morning, I woke before everyone else and moved to the window. The communities an hour outside Prague had a distinct look and feel that took me back to my time in former East Germany two years earlier. It seemed as if time had stood still and the villages remained stuck in the 1970s.

The train pulled into the central station in Prague seven years after the fall of communism, but it felt like seven days. Shades of brown and smoky gray dominated the buildings, and the smell of diesel fuel stung my nose. Even the air felt heavier as we climbed the stairs to the sunlight and took our first steps onto the cobblestone streets. The shops looked rundown, and the people loitering on the corners seemed a little seedy. I wondered whether my persistence to visit Prague had been wise, but as we kept walking, the shops brightened and the residents smiled when we passed them on the sidewalk. I let out a loud sigh.

We searched for a place to stay near Old Town Square and found a cheap hotel—and by cheap, I mean seven-dollars-a-night cheap. Despite the price, the hotel was clean, comfortable, and only a few blocks from all the action. We dropped our bags and headed to the historic square. I could feel the pent-up energy of hope and opportunity from the city ready to explode around every new corner. All my senses were firing when I stepped onto the vast expanse of cobblestone surrounded by brilliant building facades and proud church spires. The sounds of the six-hundred-year-old Astronomical Clock and the entrepreneurial musicians playing for tourists, the smells wafting from restaurants preparing lunch, and the 360-degree views of architectural majesty had me spinning in place to capture it all.

The aromas were too much to resist, so we grabbed falafels to go before walking several blocks to Wenceslas Square, in central Prague. From there, we walked the half-mile to the famous statue of Saint Wenceslas and stood where three hundred thousand people had protested for two weeks in 1989 to end communism. It had worked, and Prague has been on track to regain its former glory ever since.

Next, we admired the crafts of local artisans as we crossed Charles Bridge and headed through the arch of the bridge tower. We navigated our way up the narrow cobblestone streets until we hit lush green gardens outside Prague Castle. We rested under a canopy of trees with branches providing shade to weary travelers. Once we recharged, I found an overlook with a 180-degree view of Prague and the rolling hills around it.

Prague Castle—and its cathedral, St. Vitus—at the summit of the hill was our ultimate destination, and it was worth every step. In front of me were the Gothic spires and Romanesque towers of the largest ancient castle in the world. Behind me was Charles Bridge, crossing over the Vltava River, and Prague, extending for miles before giving way to the countryside full of trees changing from their summer foliage to their brilliant fall colors. At that moment, I knew why so many people said Prague was the most beautiful city in Europe.

This was the experience I'd needed—not another beer or party, but culture and beauty. Prague delivered that and more.

We boarded a train back to Munich early the next morning. I wished I'd allocated more time to Prague, but I didn't regret the twenty hours of train travel for twenty-four hours in the Czech Republic's capital city.

Prague must have had a similar impact on Jim because he suggested over breakfast he'd like to see more of Munich. Once I finished my baguette and stopped smiling, we walked to Marienplatz so Jim could experience the buzzing city-square Scott and I had enjoyed two years earlier. Next, we walked to the tip of the English Garden, Munich's equivalent to New York City's Central Park, and strolled along one of the forty miles of trails in the park. After lunch, we took the subway back to the Oktoberfest grounds and then patronized the Löwenbräu Brewery tent for our last night in Germany. It was a much different crowd. There was no dancing on tables or singing profanity-laden songs. Instead, we met several locals, including families with young children, during our eight-hour shift at our table. It was a relaxing, low-key last night in Munich, and I was happy.

Back in Chicago, I had only mild jet lag and plunged back into my routine of work, night classes, and socializing. Weeks after my return, I met a group of friends for dinner and drinks at a restaurant. Everyone took turns sharing memories and funny stories about college, bad dates, and travel adventures. Scott and Jim were also there, so we retold several of our tales from Oktoberfest and Prague. The story of the Germans dancing in their underwear while I pretended to be dead was always a big hit, along with the descriptions of the collective singing on tables at the Hofbräuhaus.

While someone else was sharing a less-exciting story, my friend Matt elbowed me. "Next time you guys go somewhere, let me know. I want to go too."

I nodded. "Where would you want to go?"

"I'm willing to go just about anywhere. I'm looking into Cancún right now."

I'd never been to Cancún, and the idea of heading to the Caribbean side of Mexico intrigued me. Cancun was a popular destination among friends and co-workers, and the pictures they shared upon their return of the turquoise water, rimmed by white sand beaches fueled my interest to visit.

"When do you want to go?" I asked.

"I like to go to someplace warm during the winter, so I have something to look forward to. Maybe this January or February."

He explained he'd been doing some research and found a luxury hotel in a great location at a reasonable price. It was already early November, so we'd need to book soon to get the desired rate.

Although I was just back from a major international vacation, the prospect of a warm beach in January was very appealing. I waved Jim and Scott over, and Matt shared his idea with them.

"As long as I can get the time off work, I'm in," I said. "What about you two?"

Scott shook his head. "Nah, I've got a lot going on at work at the beginning of the year, so not this time."

I looked at Jim.

"I'm in. Let's do this!"

And so, one month after returning from Oktoberfest, I booked another international flight, this time to Mexico. The act of preparing for a tropical destination was like a shot of serotonin during the long, cold, gray days of December and January in Chicago. I worked late into the evening the first three weeks in January so I wouldn't return to a mountain of work.

A week before leaving for Cancún, I met with a group of friends at a packed sports bar near my apartment. I drove by myself, intending to stay only an hour. While sitting at my table, someone caught my eye over my best friend's shoulder—a stunning young lady. She was talking with her friend, and I couldn't take my eyes off her. I caught her glancing in my direction once or twice, and I didn't hear a word my friends said after that. The urge to talk to her was so strong I worked up the nerve to say hello a few minutes later.

I strolled across the room that felt bigger than a football field, my palms sweating, and finally reached her and introduced myself. A conversation ensued with ease and she shared that her name was Sherri and that she was there with friends. Sherri was a little over five feet tall with dark brown hair, but her steel blue eyes were what nearly buckled my knees. We talked for about twenty minutes before nature called, and I excused myself to go to the bathroom.

When I returned, I saw Sherri talking to another guy and my heart sunk. I thought we were having a great conversation before I left, so this was disappointing. My first reaction was to return to my friends at the table on the other side of the dining room, but I noticed Sherri's body language gave off strong "I'm not interested" vibes—and the guy didn't seem to be getting it. So I walked back over to Sherri deciding to act as if we were old flames from high school. I figured I'd know within a second or two if she wanted to be "saved" from this guy or not.

I asked her if she still talked to the other couples who'd gone to prom with us. She immediately caught on, and together we took this guy for a ride. I asked Sherri about her sister—which she didn't have—and she asked me about my high-paying job—which I didn't have. This went on for at least five minutes, and Sherri and I really laid it on thick. We were like two seasoned improv actors in that corner of the sports bar. She got my dry sense of humor, and she had one of her own. This was the dream woman I'd been looking for—someone who appreciated my sense of humor and was also smoking hot. To me, this combination seemed as rare as a unicorn, and I considered proposing on the spot but felt it might be a tad soon. Eventually, the guy got the hint and left.

Sherri and I laughed about our ruse as the poor guy sulked on the other side of the restaurant, and then we continued talking until the bar was about to close. Feeling confident, I asked for her number.

"No," Sherri quickly replied.

"No?" I asked, to be sure I'd heard correctly.

"I don't like to talk on the phone."

The abrupt negative response shocked me, and I turned to leave, but before I took a step, I decided there was no way I was going home without her number. I turned back to Sherri and spouted a list of reasons why her giving me her number was a good idea—the first of which was that I also didn't like to talk on the phone. I'm not sure if she believed any of them or was just worn down from my persistence, but she finally caved.

I didn't play it cool and feign disinterest by waiting three days to call. I waited until I'd finished my gourmet bachelor dinner of canned ravioli the next day and called Sherri less than twenty-four hours after we met. We talked and laughed for so long my cordless phone beeped, indicating my battery was nearly dead. So much for not liking to talk on the phone.

Later that week, I asked her to go on a date that Saturday, and she said yes. After that dinner and a movie, I knew she was special. We just clicked. I didn't want the date to end, but I had to pull myself away far sooner than I wanted. I had to get up at six the next morning to catch my flight to Cancún—a trip I'd been looking forward to for the last three months. Until now.

Chapter 19

I smiled as the sun hit my cool skin outside the Cancún airport. We'd left Chicago on a bitterly wintry day, and the toasty sun and humid air were just what my body needed.

We hailed a cab, and the driver took us to the four-star resort we'd gotten for a two-star price right on the ocean along the strip. The lobby was smartly decorated, and the adjoining rooms were spacious, but the infinity pool overlooking the pale blue Caribbean Sea was the crown jewel of the property.

The three of us showered and went directly to the restaurant across the street—it was Super Bowl Sunday, and we wanted to secure a table to watch the game. The restaurant offered an all-you-can-eat taco bar, and the cocktail servers wore black-and-white-striped referee tops with whistles and carried squirt guns loaded with tequila. During commercial breaks, they'd blow their whistles, declare a penalty, and shoot tequila into your mouth for ten seconds. I tried it, realized that tequila wasn't my drink, and stuck with beer. Matt, on the other hand, committed a lot of penalties. After the game ended, the restaurant turned into a nightclub.

That's when we lost Matt.

I'd assumed he'd left with some of the people he'd been talking to during the game or had gone back to the hotel and passed out. He wasn't there when Jim and I returned, but we went to bed thinking Matt would show up later.

When we woke in the morning to find Matt wasn't in his bed, we grew concerned. Jim and I walked up and down the beach and then along the strip looking for him. When we returned to our hotel, I found a note slid under our door.

In jail

Bring money

Hurry

Those five words screamed this trip would be vastly different from any other in my life.

Our first reaction was to laugh. While looking for Matt, we'd passed a small jail with pink walls and white trim under the shade of well-manicured palm trees only five or six hotels away. It looked more like a gift shop than a menacing penitentiary, so we figured we should take our cameras and snap some photos of Matt sitting in his cell while we bailed him out.

Ten minutes later, we walked through the front door of the gift-shop jail and asked for Matt. The officer behind the counter told us he wasn't there. I asked him to check again, and he returned with the same response.

Troubled, we hurried back to the hotel and showed the concierge the note, asking him to help us find one of his incarcerated guests. He confirmed taking the call from Matt—Matt's one permitted call from jail—and agreed to help. Jim and I took a seat while he made some phone calls. I was anxious to find Matt and bail him out to find out what happened. Several minutes later, the concierge told us Matt was in the jail downtown.

That will be an even better photo op, I thought.

Jim and I considered taking the bus to save money but opted for a taxi instead since we'd never been to downtown Cancún. As we neared the city-center, I saw fewer pastel-colored hotels or souvenir shops and more locals going about their business. We were clearly out of the tourist zone when the taxi stopped in front of a municipal building, and Jim and I got out to assess the situation. As Jim brought up his camera to snap a shot of the jail for posterity's sake, a voice boomed behind us.

"Put that away! No cameras!"

We turned to find a man in military fatigues holding an AK-47.

Jim slammed the camera into his backpack, and I knew in an instant this was far more serious than we'd been taking it. I didn't want to hang around any longer than we had to after we bailed out Matt, so I asked the cab driver if he'd wait for us. He nodded, so Jim and I tiptoed inside. We approached the counter just inside the door and asked for Matt again.

A man in the police uniform walked away without saying anything, and a minute later he returned with a clear gallon bag with some personal items inside. He handed it to me, and I saw it contained Matt's wallet and belt. I was encouraged that we finally found the right location but unsure about what to do next.

"Where is Matt?" I asked.

"Go see the judge," the man in a police uniform said and moved to the other end of the counter. I looked around for a judge in a black robe but didn't see one, so I turned back to the officer and asked where I could find the judge. He pointed to an elderly man sitting at a desk across the room.

I walked over and stood over the frail man, who had only a few strands of white hair remaining. "I'm here to bail out Matt."

The judge slowly removed a notepad from his top drawer and began scribbling on it. Two lines and five minutes later, he looked up and said, "Three hundred and fifty pesos."

I opened Matt's wallet, but his driver's license was the only item remaining. Jim pretended he didn't hear the request, so I dug three hundred and fifty pesos out of my wallet—the equivalent of fifty-five US dollars at the time—laid it on the desk near the notepad, and waited while the judge counted it. He nodded and said, "Go stand by the wall."

Frustrated with the snail's pace of progress, I moved a few steps over near the wall and stood with my arms crossed. I wanted to get out of there as fast as possible but couldn't leave without Matt. Fifteen minutes later, the judge waved me back and handed me a slip of paper. "You can get him over there," he said and pointed in the direction of the police officer at the counter.

I marched back to the counter and held out the paper. "Here's the paperwork from the judge. I'm ready to take Matt."

"He's not here."

"Where is he?" I demanded. The possibility this was all a scam entered my mind. Fear and anger clashed in my stomach, but I remained calm.

He pointed outside, so I walked out and saw nothing that resembled a jail. The taxi driver intercepted me and started yelling that he'd been waiting for an hour and couldn't wait any longer. I told him we still didn't have our friend and that we couldn't leave without him. He tossed his hands into the air and stormed inside. I followed him and listened to him speak with the officer at the counter in Spanish for several minutes. Finally, he turned to Jim and me. "Let's go."

The driver spoke little English, but I managed to piece together that the downtown jail was filled to capacity thanks to the Super Bowl, and they had transferred Matt to another jail. We drove for what felt like an hour and passed through parts of Cancún I was sure no tourist had ever seen. After we bounced through a neighborhood with homes in various stages of tin-sheet and cinder-block construction, a large white building loomed outside the windshield:

Prisión de Máxima Seguridad (Maximum Security Prison).

I don't recall seeing a guard tower or fence lined with razor wire because my eyes were locked on the five or six military men with AK-47 rifles guarding the open gate.

The taxi driver stopped, and Jim immediately suggested I was far more qualified to handle the situation since I'd taken two years of Spanish in high school. I didn't argue with him. Jim agreed to stay in the car to ensure the cab was waiting when I returned with Matt. I made Jim promise three times that he wouldn't let the taxi driver leave—under any circumstances. It seemed like a simple request, but I had my concerns with Jim. He was a smart guy, but in college he had a reputation for being "laid back," but now the stakes were too high for him to assume "it's all good" and let the driver leave. My livelihood and well-being depended on Jim getting violent with the driver if necessary to prevent him from leaving, and that left a knot in my stomach. I had no idea where we were or how to get back home, and my greatest fear was to have to walk back to the main road a couple miles away to hail another taxi.

When I opened the door and exited the vehicle, I drew all the eyes and gun barrels of the prison guards. I shared my slip of paper from the judge with one of them, and he waved for me to follow him. At one point during our trek to the office, I was told to stand against a wall while a group of inmates walked by in a single file. They looked me up and down and said stuff to me in Spanish I didn't understand. I was sure it was better that I didn't know what they were saying.

We arrived at the warden's office, and the guard handed him my slip of paper. The warden read it and pointed to a chair. "Sit down."

I sat, quietly wondering when this nightmare would end as the warden flipped through papers on his desk and scribbled on each page. The only sounds were from a small black-and-white TV that flickered with an intermittent signal and a fan with steel blades slowly rotating next to me. The latter was fighting a losing battle against the dense, humid air and offered little relief. The warden's office was exactly how I'd imagined one in Mexico might look, based on a few late-night movies I'd seen.

"Hablas Español?" the warden finally asked after what felt like an eternity, although it was probably less than five minutes. He leaned forward on his desk and glared at me.

I shook my head.

"Why do you all come down here and cause trouble and not even try to speak our language?"

"I didn't come down here to cause trouble, sir. I just want to get my friend and go home, and we'll never cause any trouble again."

He searched my face, and I must have convinced him I was sincere because he made a phone call, and two minutes later, Matt walked through the door with a guard. I noticed his black eyes first, then his forearms covered in bruises, and finally the streak of dried blood stretching from his right temple down his cheek to his neck. I couldn't speak. I just stared.

"These guys beat the hell out of me!" Matt shouted when he saw me.

"Shut up!" I hissed, just wanting to get out of there.

"It's police brutality, and I'm not going to let them get away with it," Matt ranted, like a hardened criminal.

"Let's go."

The guard led us out of the warden's office to the gate where I left Jim. I was never so happy to see a corn yellow taxi waiting for me. Once the prison was several blocks behind us, I exhaled with relief and peppered Matt with questions.

"What happened?"

"They just grabbed me and started beating me. After they beat me, they took all my money. Then, in the middle of the night, they put a couple other guys and me in the back of a pickup truck with a German shepherd and took us to the prison. They said if I moved the dog would attack."

"Why did they grab you?"

"Because I'm an American," Matt stated dryly, which was the last thing I'd wanted to hear. The cab was quiet for the rest of the trip back to the hotel.

This certainly wasn't the relaxing vacation I'd envisioned when I landed in Cancún twenty-four hours earlier. Now I had to watch my back so I wouldn't end up beaten and imprisoned like Matt.

Chapter 20

The pool and the on-site restaurant were the only places we frequented for the next two days, out of fear of being plucked off the streets by rogue police officers. Matt stuck with his story that he was an innocent victim, so I didn't want to risk leaving the grounds.

At the end of those two days, I'd tired of spending every waking hour on the same pool deck, so I returned to the concierge and asked about excursions. He rattled off several options with jet skis, snorkeling, and boats, including the popular booze cruise, but I opted for the bus to Chichen Itza, the site of the ancient Mayan ruins and pyramids several hours inland. I hoped getting away from Cancún for a day would get my mind off an unwanted encounter with the police holding me hostage at the resort. An epic historic site might be just what I needed to inflate my mood.

During dinner, I asked Jim and Matt if they wanted to go. Matt replied with a quick yes, but unsurprisingly, Jim, of "never leave the Hofbräuhaus tent at Oktoberfest" fame, said he'd prefer to stay back and hang out by the pool.

The next day, Matt and I boarded the charter bus for the journey into the lowland forests of the Yucatán Peninsula. Our excursion included a guided tour of the grounds and buildings within the one-thousand-year-old Mayan city. The guide explained the cultural and ritual uses of each building and took us to a grassy court where they'd played a game like handball. It sounded fun until she shared the losing team was usually decapitated as an offering to the evil spirits.

After the tour, Matt and I climbed the pyramids and walked the grounds of the ancient great civilization. As I'd hoped, Chichen Itza was exactly what I'd needed. Walking on the same turf, running my fingers along the same stories etched in stone, and viewing the jungle from the tops of the same pyramids as the Maya had millennia earlier refilled my bucket. It was my Prague moment in Mexico.

During the long bus ride back to our hotel, Matt turned to me with a blank look on his face. "I think I may have deserved what happened to me."

I frowned. "What do you mean?"

"I remember more now. I wasn't just randomly pulled off the street and arrested because I was American."

I remained quiet as I sensed a confession coming.

"Now I remember that I left the restaurant we were at with some other people, and when I tried to get back in, the bouncer said I'd had too much to drink. I tried to push past him, and then he pushed me, so I punched him. We started punching each other, and that's when I felt somebody grab me from behind. I thought it was another bouncer, so I turned around and punched him too, but it wasn't a bouncer—it was a cop. After I punched him, he pulled out his baton and started hitting me. Another cop came over and started hitting me too. That's why I have all these bruises on my forearms." Matt rose his arms to prove his point.

"You just remembered this now?" I asked as I adjusted the collar of my polo shirt and rubbed the back of my neck. I suddenly felt warm.

"Yeah, everything from that night is still pretty blurry. I'm pretty sure I have a concussion."

I looked at the gash on his temple and nodded. "Matt, they would have thrown you in jail in the US if you did that. What did you think was going to happen?"

"I know. I wasn't thinking at the time. I just wanted you to know that the cops aren't pulling Americans off the street, beating them, and throwing them in jail. I guess I kind of deserved it."

I turned away from Matt and looked out the window the rest of the way to our hotel. Although I was irritated and annoyed with Matt for the three days we wasted thinking the police were plucking innocent Americans off the street, those feelings dissipated and turned to relief. Now we could leave the resort and resume our Caribbean vacation before returning to frigid Chicago.

Back at the hotel, Matt told Jim the complete story as well. We had only three nights remaining, and we all wanted to make up for lost time, but I was still a little hesitant to get too crazy in the bars and clubs of Cancún. Guards with AK-47s and the warden's office were still fresh in my mind. After batting around a few options, we agreed the booze cruise would be the safest way to let loose.

As we set out for the ticket office the next day, a guy on the street stopped us. He had a fistful of tickets for various excursions and asked if we wanted discount prices. We were about to walk away when he mentioned the booze cruise—it was half-price.

All of us pulled out our wallets and paid the discounted fee for a cruise later that evening. We received our tickets and complimented ourselves on our luck finding half-price tickets while on our way to pay full price. We hung out on the beach until it was time to get ready for the sunset cruise.

After we'd put on our finest booze-cruise attire of Hawaiian shirts and cargo shorts, we took a bus to the designated dock. I noticed a long line of people as soon as we stepped off the bus. I checked my ticket and confirmed we were departing from the same dock as a hundred or more thirsty individuals. We found our place in the back of the line, and before long, a two-story yacht—about the size of a classic Mississippi riverboat, with lights flashing and music pumping—pulled up. The line shrunk as the excited partygoers found their way onto the ship. Finally, when it was our turn, the person taking the tickets looked at ours twice and called for someone else to come over. That person looked at our tickets and said, "I'm sorry, this isn't your boat. Yours will arrive soon."

I was disappointed but not alarmed. It made sense the entire line of people wouldn't fit on that yacht. Until they all did. Only one other guy was waiting for the next boat with Matt, Jim, and me. The booze cruise drifted away, and soon the laughter and flashing lights vanished into the dark. Ten minutes later, another boat arrived.

It was a fishing boat about one hundred times smaller than the exquisite vessel that had recently left.

The six crewmates on the fishing boat all had toothy grins and waved for us to board. We hesitated.

"I don't think this is the booze cruise we wanted," I told Jim and Matt.

"Yeah, but we already paid for the tickets," Jim said. "Maybe we should go."

Matt and I thought about it and agreed getting on a strange boat in which we'd be outnumbered by the crew to sail into the ocean in a foreign country in the dark made perfect sense because we'd already invested seventy-five dollars each. We boarded the open-air boat and sat quietly as the captain idled through the harbor. The booze cruise had turned south toward the hotel zone after it departed, but our craft turned north into the pitch-black gulf. The air suddenly felt colder. I watched the lights of Cancún dip below the swells. Nobody spoke. The only sound was the wind, the hum of the engine, and occasional laughter from the crew.

Fifteen minutes into our journey, a member of the crew approached us. "Do you know where we are going tonight?"

Jim, Matt, and I shook our heads in unison.

"We are going to Cuba."

My heart sank. I tried to mentally calculate if I could make it to shore if I jumped out now. Could I swim that far? Would sharks get me first? Why hadn't I just paid full price for the real booze cruise?

The entire crew laughed. The looks on our faces must have screamed we were beyond terrified.

I kept my eyes locked on the direction we were heading through the captain's windshield. Soon I saw lights and then the outline of a small island. My pulse slowed as I became less concerned about finding a ride back from Cuba, but I was still apprehensive about what was on that island.

We tied off at a wooden dock next to three other boats and followed the crew members to a building that still smelled like fresh paint. They guided us inside to a large room with tables and a stage. Everything sparkled under the bright lights and pastel green, yellow, blue and red the dominant colors. A man in a suit walked on stage and leaned into a microphone to address the fifteen other guests seated around Jim, Matt, and me.

"Welcome to the celebration of Havana. Please grab a plate and eat."

My concern turned to excitement.

The crew member had only been partially joking. We learned this was a new banquet facility owned by a hotel and restaurant group from Cuba to showcase their food, dancing, and music. For the next two hours, the group of twenty or so performed for their first paying guests. The spread at the buffet was terrific, and at one point we even joined some of the beautiful dancers dressed in traditional Cuban garb on stage. Despite my near heart attack, I ended up enjoying the night and earned a suspenseful story I'll tell until I die.

We stayed on the resort the last two days, other than for a quick excursion to snorkel along the reef. I'd had enough excitement in Mexico and was ready to return home. This time, I wasn't homesick. I was Sherri-sick. I hadn't been able to stop thinking about that perfect date we'd had a week earlier. During the entire flight home, I worried Sherri had forgotten about me, or worse—that she wouldn't want to talk to me anymore.

Chapter 21

"You're already back?" Sherri asked when I called her ten minutes after arriving back in my apartment. All that worry, and she'd barely noticed my absence.

Relief swept over me, and we talked late into the night about my trip. The call ended with a plan for a second date. That date ended with another date, and I fell hard for the blue-eyed beauty with chestnut-brown hair.

Days turned to weeks, weeks turned to months, and before I knew it, we'd been dating a couple of years. I still wanted to travel extensively, especially to Europe, but the lure to "settle down" in a stable relationship was also strong. Plus, it seemed Sherri and I enjoyed many of the same things, including travel, so I felt we could be in a serious relationship and still keep my wanderlust dreams alive. While we weren't traveling, I wanted to get more "established" with housing and income, so I purchased my first home in Schaumburg, Illinois in the northwest suburbs of Chicago and transitioned to a higher paying job closer to my new two-bedroom condo. Sherri and I spent most of our free time together as we enjoyed the amenities of downtown Chicago, thirty miles east of where we lived. Sporting events, restaurants, Lake Michigan, neighborhood street festivals, and live-performance theaters were often on our agenda when we'd go out on an extra-special date. But on most dates, we'd meet friends at a restaurant or catch a movie closer to where we lived.

Shortly after Christmas, we took our first major trip together, to Miami, Florida. We always had a great time with each other but rarely discussed what we wanted for our futures. I hoped the trip would offer some clarity.

On New Year's Eve, we watched the fireworks from a boat in Miami harbor, and the next day, we watched the college bowl games from an outdoor patio at a restaurant in Fort Lauderdale. I'd been thinking about taking the next step in our relationship and wanted to confirm Sherri and I were on the same page on important topics like having kids, traveling and where to live. I'd save the discussion on kids for another day, but on the patio that evening, I opened up and shared my strong desire to travel.

"I hope we can take several more vacations this year."

"Me too," Sherri replied as she kept her eyes on the TV.

"I'd like to go to some new and interesting places. Is there anywhere special you'd like to go?"

Sherri shook her head. "Nope. I'm willing to go about anywhere as long as it's safe and you plan it."

That was the type of answer I was hoping to hear, but that was only my baby reveal. Next, I floated an idea I'd been kicking around for several months. During a commercial break, I turned to Sherri. "I don't want to go back. It's so nice down here."

"I know. I hate the snow and cold."

"I could live down here."

"Me too."

I leaned closer to her. "I'm serious. I've always wanted to live somewhere warmer, so I'd have no problem moving from Chicago down here." I watched her carefully, gauging her reaction.

"I've been coming down here once a year for most of my life. I could easily move here."

A wide smile formed on my face. "Want to check out the area more tomorrow and see if we could really live here?"

She agreed, and the following day, we drove our rental car all over Southeast Florida with a potential move in mind. That afternoon, we met Sherri's uncle, whose house was backed up to a canal connected to the Intracoastal Waterway. He asked if we wanted to go for a ride, and twenty minutes later, I was a mile off the coast of Fort Lauderdale in the Atlantic Ocean. The experience sold me on moving to Florida.

We returned home to several feet of snow, and our focus turned to moving to the Sunshine State. I was pleased with this shift—moving would also fulfill my desire to explore and investigate. As the snow melted and the days grew longer, I began thinking about another trip high on my priority list. I'd wanted to go to a Chicago Cubs spring training game in Mesa since I was in the first grade. I told Sherri about my desire to fly to Arizona to scratch this itch, but she wasn't interested. She'd never been to Arizona and wasn't too keen on visiting a desert. She was "more of a beach girl," she said. Plus, she didn't like the idea of spending every afternoon at a baseball game.

This led to one of our first big fights.

I wanted to go badly enough I threatened to go alone. That was a rookie move, and after we'd both taken a couple of days to cool down, I cut down the baseball games to one day, and Sherri joined me on my bucket-list trip.

We stayed at a luxurious resort at South Mountain in Phoenix and visited the touristy areas of Tempe, Scottsdale, and Phoenix. We attended the Chicago Cubs spring training game and I loved the relaxed atmosphere and interaction with the players in the smaller, more intimate stadium. After the game, we enjoyed delicious Mexican food under the stars while a snowstorm raged in Chicago. During that week in the desert, Sherri formed a much better impression of it.

Over the summer, we continued to discuss a move to South Florida, but despite looking every day, I had no luck finding a suitable job or housing in a location we desired. That's when I floated a new destination to Sherri.

"What about adding Arizona as an option?" I asked.

"It was nice, but I still don't know much about it," she said. "I've been to Miami so many times and already know my way around the area a little. Plus, my uncle lives there, so Florida is still where I'd prefer to move."

The only houses we could afford in Florida were many miles from the beach, and that was if I could get a job making the same salary I earned in Chicago. It didn't look promising for a marketing manager for a consumer products company. But Sherri was more comfortable with Florida, so I kept trying.

A couple of weeks later, I pushed myself away from my computer in frustration and called Sherri. "I want to go back to Arizona this fall."

"I thought we agreed to keep looking at Florida."

"I'm still looking at Florida for jobs and houses, but I'd like to go to the Grand Canyon, Sedona, and see more of Scottsdale for a vacation. Plus, your aunt just moved out there, so we can visit her too."

The line was quiet for several seconds. "I've always wanted to see the Grand Canyon."

And so, in early October we flew to Phoenix, rented a car, and drove five hours north to the Grand Canyon. We watched two breathtaking sunsets from the South Rim where pictures or words could never do it justice. You have to see it for yourself. Next, we drove two hours south. I'm sure my mouth was wide open from the top of Oak Creek Canyon all the way to the southern boundary of Sedona. It was a natural beauty I'd never witnessed anywhere in my life, and it left me speechless. The combination of rugged red rocks of all shapes and sizes blanketed by low-slung juniper trees and towering ponderosa pines was stunning. Add the trout-filled, tree-lined Oak Creek meandering through its namesake canyon and the Sedona Valley and you have a recipe for ten-out-of-ten stars of awe-inspiring scenery.

We rented a hotel in Sedona with a fireplace, but I didn't want to be inside much, so we hiked, shopped, and dined on outdoor patios while watching the sun set and the full moon rise over the tree-lined red mountains. After Sedona, we spent several days in the Valley of the Sun. We explored the popular shopping and dining haunts of Scottsdale and walked along Tempe Town Lake. Sherri called her aunt that had recently moved to the far northeastern corner of Mesa from the Chicago area to see if we could coordinate a time to meet up with her. Her aunt invited us over for dinner, so the next evening we drove to her home in Mesa.

As we chatted around the dinner table, Sherri's aunt asked us to guess the value of her home, which had three bedrooms, two bathrooms, and a garage, as well as a pool, which we happened to be swimming in. At first, I was shocked by the personal question, but curiosity took over, and I rendered an estimate based on my limited knowledge of the Chicago housing market in early 2000. She smiled and said she and her boyfriend had paid less than half that amount. Within seconds, Arizona claimed sole possession on my list of destinations I wanted to move to. Sherri was equally surprised and impressed.

There was only one major problem. Sherri was still my girlfriend, and I wouldn't move across the country to buy a home with a girlfriend. By this point, we'd been dating for over three years, and I knew I wanted to spend the rest of my life with her, so I went shopping for rings and found the princess-cut diamond on the platinum band Sherri had been subtly mentioning over the previous few months. I made payments on the ring while I considered the right time and place to pop the question. I wanted the proposal to be epic—one we'd both remember forever. A few weeks later, I picked a date and began preparing my grand proposal, but I never got the chance to implement it. Life had a different plan for me.

Chapter 22

I'd just finished a high-carb lunch and my eyes were growing heavy when my boss walked up to my cubicle and stood over my desk.

"You got a minute?" Eric asked.

"Sure."

"Let's go into my office."

I followed Eric and settled myself in a comfortable chair from which I had stellar views out of his office window, perched in the corner of the fourteenth floor in the northwest suburbs of Chicago. The only view from my cubicle was of an eggshell-white wall, but Eric enjoyed the sight of a fountain in the middle of a modest lake surrounded by impeccably landscaped buildings in the office complex.

It wasn't unusual for Eric to invite me to his office. We had a relationship built on mutual respect and often went out together for lunch. Occasionally, he recruited me to be his partner in crime for extended lunch hours that included the driving range, bowling, and one trip to buy his son a new baseball cap—thirty miles away at Wrigley Field, home of the Chicago Cubs baseball team, in Chicago.

Eric was a great boss and I trusted him, yet I clutched the arms of the chair while he fidgeted at his desk. He was acting peculiar, and that gave me the feeling something was up.

Finally, after several seconds of awkward silence, he looked up. "Do you have a passport?"

"Yes, I do." Where was this going?

"How would you like to go to Malaysia with me?"

I tried to respond with a level of excitement because I could sense it was a big deal to Eric. "I'd love to go," I lied.

Although I was comfortable with international travel, Asia was in an entirely new league. While many of the places I'd visited in Europe had felt like the Northeastern United States with a twist, Asia seemed like a truly foreign land. It intimidated me and therefore its countries had never made it onto my list of must-see destinations.

At this time, I worked for a personal protective equipment company, which is a fancy way of saying we made latex gloves for the healthcare industry. We were owned by a British firm with manufacturing facilities in Kuala Lumpur, Malaysia—near the source of the natural rubber latex. During my first eighteen months at the company, the only person to travel to Malaysia had been the president, and that had only happened once, so I'd never expected I'd have to go. The only thing I knew about Malaysia was that it was on the opposite side of the globe and the recently constructed Petronas Towers had surpassed the Sears Tower in Chicago (Willis Tower today) to become the tallest buildings in the world.

Eric explained we'd be presenting at a global branding summit the day after we arrived, and then we'd tour the manufacturing facilities in the area. We had four weeks to prepare our presentation and travel plans.

I grew anxious every time I thought about the trip. My proposal to Sherri was put on hold as I developed my presentation and booked my flight and hotel. The thought of the long flight over the Pacific was one source of my anxiety, but mainly I was nervous about the food and cultural differences. Although my palate was expanding with more than foods found in American households, I still wasn't comfortable with the intense seafood and vegetable diets I understood were common in Southeast Asia. I also wasn't sure if rejecting local cuisine in favor of a juicy cheeseburger was considered good etiquette for a guest in Malaysia.

On departure day, my boss Eric and I flew from Chicago to Los Angeles, where I boarded a Singapore Airlines 747 and found my seat in business class. I'd never been in business class in a three-class jet before, and it was better than I'd expected. There were seven seats in a row versus the eleven I'd experienced on previous international flights, and the plush seats reclined at least a foot. I was grateful my company's policy was to book business-class seats on flights over ten hours. The next leg, to Taipei, Taiwan, was over twelve hours.

In Taipei, Eric and I explored the airport, and five hours later, we landed in Singapore. We rushed to a locker to secure our belongings as soon as the cabin door opened. We had a seven-hour layover in the bustling city-state and wanted to travel light to see as much as possible.

We didn't have a plan, so we took a cab to Orchard Plaza, located near museums, restaurants, and a mall. The goal was to walk around and soak up some of the local culture, but it became apparent this was a bad idea as soon as we exited the cab. Singapore is only one degree north of the equator and is exceptionally humid. I'd thought the humidity in Florida was oppressive, but it's nothing like Singapore's 24/7 steam-bath conditions. The air was soupy, and I started to sweat within a minute or two of our walk.

It was near lunchtime, so I convinced Eric to duck inside a restaurant to get out of the heat and enjoy our first meal on the Malay Peninsula. I devoured a barbecue chicken pizza, my usual favorite at California Pizza Kitchen. Authentic cuisine would have to wait until dinner.

After lunch, we walked a bit more, then took a cab to a hotel in downtown Singapore, at the top of which was a restaurant. I took pictures of the clean, modern structures surrounded by green, flowering plants and general natural beauty. It was easy to understand the appeal of Singapore.

The high heat index having zapped our energy, Eric and I went back to the airport an hour early. I approached the check-in counter and proudly pulled out my paper ticket from my fanny pack. The man looked at the ticket and smiled. I smiled back.

"Your passport?" he asked.

My heart sunk and I turned to Eric in a panic. "Our passports. We locked them up on the other side of security."

My mind immediately went to the American teenager sentenced to six strokes of the cane in Singapore in 1994 for vandalizing cars. The beating had left him bloodied despite the sentence being reduced to four strokes. How many strokes would I get for the lack of a passport?

Seeing I was frozen with fear, Eric stepped up and explained the situation. We were moved to a private room, where we listened to several lectures on the importance of keeping our passports "on our person at all times" before security allowed us to pass through and catch our flight to Kuala Lumpur. It was a good thing we'd arrived early.

The global branding summit started the following day. Eric and I presented our brand plan in the afternoon. We were both armed with engaging slides and compelling insights that appeared to be well-received by the global audience. After the summit, we joined our Malaysian marketing peers at the resort restaurant serving dim sum, a traditional Chinese meal made up of small plates of appetizers, dumplings, and seafood, similar to Spanish tapas. The small plates were on a lazy Susan in the middle of our round table for eight. I spun it and grabbed every plate of shrimp tempura I could locate. It was the only item on the table I could identify with a high degree of confidence and therefore the safest option for me. Although I was still hungry after finishing the shrimp, I drew attention to myself by resisting the recommendations of a local marketing manager to try other items on the rotating tray. He stared in my direction until dinner was over.

Four hours after I went to bed, I woke starving. The clock radio near my bed said 3:04 a.m., but my body thought it was the middle of the afternoon because of the twelve-hour time difference. I meandered down to the resort's twenty-four-hour buffet and gorged myself on fried chicken and a side of macaroni and cheese. Despite slight indigestion, I was content.

The next day, we moved from the posh resort outside the city to a five-star hotel in the center of Kuala Lumpur, or KL as the locals call it. The hotel had an infinity pool on the sixth floor and shared a property line with the Petronas Towers. I stared at the eighty-eight-story twin towers with spires rising nearly fifteen hundred feet in the sky from the bed in my hotel room each night.

For the next three days, we visited factories and rubber plantations on the outskirts of the city. I was impressed with the new knowledge of extracting the yellow-white natural rubber latex from hevea brasiliensis trees but appalled at the near-subsistence level conditions of the plantation workers that tap the trees twice a day. Entire families live in one-room tin huts on the plantation with a few chickens or a goat to earn an annual income less than my hotel bill for a week in Malaysia. The plantation manager and guide told Eric and I the number one cause of death for workers were cobra bites. I never took my eyes off the ground the rest of the tour after learning that fact.

We spent our evenings dining in and exploring more of metro Kuala Lumpur. One evening after dinner, we visited the famous Taman Connaught Night Market in the heart of KL. The toys, DVDs, and electronic gadgets were similar to items I'd seen in the United States—as were several food items, such as dumplings, desserts, and cooked meats on sticks. Then it got interesting.

I turned down a row crowded with local shoppers and saw raw fish, shrimp, and eels in the first booth. The next booth had a variety of insects, such as crickets and grasshoppers, available for purchase either raw or roasted. I passed a few more seafood booths, then came to a vendor with baskets filled with hundreds of snakes, more eels, and scorpions on a stick. At the end of the row were a dozen tanks filled with live fish. The booth owners plucked them out with a net and passed them in clear bags to patrons, just like at pet stores in the US. Except these fish wouldn't be transitioning to a tank with colorful gravel, filter, and a plastic scuba diver—they'd be dinner for a family. All the sights, sounds, and smells made my heart race. The market felt like a microcosm of food and culture in Malaysia, and I got a full-immersion crash course under the moon and stars. At the end of the row, I was both queasy and delighted. It confirmed my cautious approach to Malay cuisine was warranted, while I also relished the opportunity to experience the unique food options firsthand.

On our second-to-last night, we met with the local marketing managers again at another restaurant that served dim sum. This time, the manager I'd thwarted earlier in the week was ready for me. He locked his gaze on me as I filled my plate with more shrimp tempura.

"Come on, try something new," he bellowed from across the table.

"I will," I lied. "Shrimp tempura is my favorite, though."

To relieve myself from the heat of his gaze, I spun the lazy Susan around and grabbed a dumpling. It was a safe choice but one I hoped would satisfy the man. It didn't.

"That's dessert. Don't be a chicken. Try some real Malay food."

The lazy Susan stopped in front of me again, and this time I selected a plate of tempura vegetables. They weren't too bad, so I tried another plate of dumplings with a chopped meat and vegetable filling.

Just as I was gaining a little confidence and felt I could expand my palate a bit more, the manager took control of the lazy Susan and spun it until a specific plate was in front of me.

"Try that."

It looked like some type of fried calamari. I'd tried calamari a couple of times and liked it, so I picked up a piece and bit into it. It felt as if my front teeth had hit a bone, so I immediately pulled it out of my mouth.

"No, no, no!" the manager shrieked. "Bite it, hold, and then pull off the meat."

I paused, looked around the table at all the eyes on me, and did as he suggested. Both the texture and the taste nearly made me gag. I didn't want to be rude, though, so I took a drink to swallow what was still in my mouth.

All the Malaysians at the table erupted in laughter.

"What was that?"

"Chicken foot!" one howled.

That settled it. I would have to survive on a diet of shrimp tempura and the bags of trail mix the hotel staff left in my room each day.

My suspension of food anxiety was short-lived. On our last evening in Malaysia, Eric and I had dinner with the president of the US division and the CEO of the global organization. This time it wouldn't be at a dim-sum restaurant but a fine-dining establishment.

Once the four of us found our seats, I scanned the menu. The CEO, a soft-spoken Chinese man, noticed and said, "Please allow me to order for the table." I put down my menu, bowed my head, and said a silent prayer he loved shrimp tempura.

The CEO ordered in Chinese, and my stomach did somersaults while I waited to see what dishes would show up. I had visions of the scorpions and snakes at the night market and shuddered.

The first item to arrive was a green salad with ginger dressing that looked like something I'd eat back home. My heart rate slowed a bit while I ate it and listened to the conversation among the other three at the table. I tried to pretend I was interested, but I was really watching our server go into and out of the kitchen to see what was on his tray.

Twenty minutes later, our server exited the kitchen doors with four plates. As he got closer, I saw the items. I didn't have time for a silent prayer and instead blurted out, "Please God, don't let this be our tray."

My prayer was not answered. The server placed a plate in front of me, and my pulse quickened. I stared at my dish, and it stared back at me. It was a whole fish, complete with its skin, tail, head, and eyes. It looked as if it had jumped right out of the water and onto my plate. When it came to seafood, all I'd eaten at this point in my life were heavily breaded fish sticks, lobster drowned in butter, fried shrimp, and calamari (a couple of times).

The CEO raised his wine glass for a toast. "Thank you for traveling all the way from the United States and spending the week with us. I hope you found your experience beneficial, and I hope you enjoy the fish I ordered for all of us tonight. It's a delicacy in Malaysia, and it's my favorite."

Not wanting to be disrespectful, I pretended to be very interested in my wine while watching the other three take a bite. Nobody winced or gagged, so I cut off a small piece of flesh from behind the dorsal fin and put it in my mouth. I chewed slowly and noticed the CEO was looking at me.

"What do you think?"

"It's excellent," I replied, and it wasn't a lie. Despite its appearance, the fish tasted amazing. "What is it?" I asked after taking another bite.

"It's a freshwater fish called empurau."

I later learned it was one of the most expensive fish in Malaysia. Empurau are known for their sweet, tender flesh because of their diet of fruits and flowers. At the time, it wasn't uncommon to see empurau cost over one hundred US dollars at a restaurant in Kuala Lumpur.

Minutes later, I'd devoured the entire fish. Not only did I have a full belly, but I also felt full of accomplishment. I'd overcome my fear of unfamiliar foods.

That fish taught me so much. It taught me I'd never experience the richness of life if I didn't try new things.

It taught me fear was a prison and only I had the keys to let myself out. It taught me I'd miss out on the things in life that mattered to me most if I kept putting everything off. I know that's a lot to learn from a one-pound fish, but it's true.

On my way back to the hotel that night, I decided to stop trying to prepare the ultimate proposal for Sherri and just pop the question. She was the most important person in my life. I couldn't delay any longer.

Chapter 23

Four months after I returned from Malaysia, I planned to pop the question, so I invited Sherri over for dinner. I'd made her favorite meal—grilled lobster tail with asparagus—and spread red rose petals on the carpet of my condo. I'd even purchased those stainless-steel butter warmers heated with tea-light candles.

When she arrived, I got down on one knee, and with the support of my red Doberman puppy, Daylie, I opened the ring box to show her the princess-cut diamond on a platinum band. She took a lot longer than I'd expected to answer. The memory of the first time I asked for her phone number flashed through my mind, but she eventually said yes.

"Are you sure? You hesitated for a second there," I asked hoping for a more confident response.

"Yes. Yes, I'm sure. I wasn't expecting this and you caught me off guard."

Sherri, Daylie, and I would be a family.

For the next several days, we drove to visit friends and family to share the news in person. My new fiancée (it was so fun to say "fiancée" for the first few days!) and I discussed venue options for the wedding. I have a very large extended family. My mom is one of thirteen children, and my dad is one of nine, which means I have nearly one hundred aunts, uncles and first cousins, and that didn't include any friends. Sherri and I both wanted a smaller, more intimate wedding, and we loved her brother's wedding on the shore of Lake Tahoe a year earlier, so we agreed on a destination wedding with immediate family and close friends. I took on the task of finding the wedding location, venue, and rehearsal dinner site while Sherri took the lead on flowers, cake, and invitations. We each shared a verbal list of "must-haves" for a venue, and this narrowed down the location to a few places on the California coast. We ended up choosing a lush and charming Mediterranean-style resort on the beach in Santa Barbara, California.

I'd never been to Santa Barbara before, but the pictures on the hotel website looked spectacular, and I was excited I had a reason to visit the Central Coast. We flew from Chicago to Santa Barbara three times over the next few months to work with the resort catering and event team to select our venue layout and food options. We also found local vendors for our cake, flowers, pastor, photographer, and tuxedo rental. For the rehearsal dinner, we chose a seafood restaurant near the pier. The entire process was smooth and gratifying to complete alongside my future wife.

Last, Sherri purchased her dress at a shop in Chicago, and we counted down the days. About three weeks before our wedding, I called all the suppliers, vendors, and service providers to verify everything would be ready to go. To my dismay, the restaurant I'd selected for the rehearsal dinner wouldn't answer the phone or return my daily messages. Desperate, I called a business next door and asked if the seafood restaurant was still open, and they said it had closed a month ago.

I panicked and scoured the Internet for days to find a suitable replacement. Nobody had room for our party of thirty guests on such short notice. I was about ready to call an international pancake chain restaurant to see if they could accommodate us when I received a call back from a chef in the neighboring town of Montecito.

The chef of the fine-dining Italian restaurant assured me in her Ethiopian accent she'd take care of our rehearsal dinner. I clarified several times that our wedding party was from the Midwest and we wanted nothing too eccentric. Just basic Italian fare. She told me to leave it all up to her. Every fiber in my control-freak being told me I had to help select the appetizers and main course, but the chef wouldn't even entertain it. My positive experience with trying new foods in Malaysia made me less resistant to the chef selecting the items on our menu, but I was still concerned with my dad. If pickiness is inherited, then I got it from him. He eats a limited rotation of basic meals and thinks everything is spicy. One day when my parents were over at my condo in Schaumburg, I grilled plain chicken breasts for sandwiches. I added provolone cheese and barbeque sauce to provide some flavor. After I served the sandwiches, I watched my dad take a bite, then heard him yell one second later.

"What's wrong? Did you bite into something?" I quickly asked.

"No! This barbeque sauce is too spicy. You know I can't eat stuff this spicy!" he yelled in a tone that brought me back to many of my scoldings during my youth.

"What kind is this?"

I went into the kitchen and grabbed the bottle.

"It's Kraft Original Barbeque Sauce."

That's why I was concerned the Chef may not understand the level of blandness I was targeting for some guests. After my conversation with the Chef, I told Sherri I'd found a new venue but lied and said I'd helped pick the menu and had everything under control. I frequently prayed for everything to work out.

The night before our wedding, we arrived early at the restaurant in the village of Montecito. Sherri questioned the eclectic menu the chef had prepared for us while my stomach did flips. I watched our guests closely as the staff served their meals. Several bites later, I saw nods and even a few smiles.

Afterward, everyone raved about the food, and I thanked the chef for helping me out of my comfort zone. That's when I learned she'd trained at Michelin-star restaurants in Italy and was a favorite chef of several local celebrities. I couldn't believe my good fortune. I'd found one of the best restaurants in the area in the Yellow Pages weeks before my wedding and received praise from my future wife and guests for finding such a gem.

The wedding ceremony took place under a threatening gray sky on an enclosed patio whose low walls were covered in flowering vines. Cool mist had alternated with intermittent rain all morning but stopped minutes before the ceremony that May afternoon. Forty-five minutes later, I was a married man, and Sherri was my wife.

We treated our guests to a reception in a room overlooking the dunes and white sand of East Beach and then a trolley ride through the hills of Santa Barbara. Since it was a destination wedding, we delayed a full honeymoon and instead spent a couple of days on Catalina Island, thirty miles off the California coast. Three days after our wedding, we returned to our lives in Chicago, where Sherri moved into my condo with Daylie and me and we started our lives as a family. I was eager to explore new travel and relocation destinations with my wife and best friend.

Sherri and I looked at each other to see who would reveal the news. Three months had passed, and we'd gathered our immediate families at a restaurant to make the big announcement. Our mothers smiled at us, signaling they were ready to accept the title of grandparents. I cleared my throat to speak, and the smiles vanished and jaws dropped when instead I told them we were moving to Arizona. We'd purchased a home during a recent weekend trip to Phoenix, and we'd be moving in less than a month.

It felt as if the air had been sucked from the room.

My mother-in-law said "What? Why?" a few times while processing news far different from what she'd expected.

Sherri and I hadn't intentionally kept our plans to move a secret; everything had just happened much faster than anticipated. Our weekend trip to Phoenix the previous week was supposed to have been a recon excursion to determine if we liked any of the neighborhoods with houses in our price range to help narrow our search, which we expected to take months or even years. We drove through a neighborhood with palm-tree-lined streets and lakes, on which boats were docked behind the homes we couldn't afford. We fell in love with the community, though, and on a street one hundred yards from the nearest lake, we drove past a home three times larger than my condo that had lemon trees in the back and a For Sale sign in the front. Our real estate agent warned us it may take several rounds of negotiation to finalize an agreement, so we made an offer that night. Shockingly, they accepted, and we were future homeowners of a house in Arizona before we boarded our flight home.

Eventually, the shock of our announcement wore off, and our parents were supportive of the move. I sold my condo and packed our yellow Ryder truck for the fifteen-hundred-mile drive to the Phoenix area. We would take possession of our new home in three days, and I couldn't wait to walk through the front door of my first single family home.

On September 11, 2001, I woke up in my condo for the last time and got ready to attend the signing of the closing documents with my attorney before Sherri and I started our trek to Arizona. While getting ready for the day, I walked past a TV that was on in the adjacent family room and fell limp into my couch when I saw one of the World Trade Center towers burning. The news anchors debated the cause of the fire while I tried to process the situation. During their debate, a news camera caught a plane flying into the other tower. The anchors fell silent, and a chill thrust up my spine. I knew we were under attack by terrorists. Minutes later, the newscast confirmed hijackers had taken over the planes. The chaos continued. A third plane crashed into the Pentagon, and then United Airlines flight 93 crashed into a field in Pennsylvania.

I watched the TV in horror while one of the pundits said the towers could collapse from the intense fire. I wanted those towers to remain standing with every fiber of my being—not only to preserve thousands of lives but also to symbolize America could withstand such an attack. I watched the South Tower wobble and then fall—a tower I'd been in with Sherri nine months earlier on a business trip to New York City. A lump formed in my throat and stayed there as the North Tower hung on for another twenty-nine minutes before collapsing as well. I've never felt so vulnerable and helpless in my life.

Not sure what to do next, I paced my condo in a fog. Innocent civilians were under attack from international terrorists, and I was moving away from family and friends. My move to Arizona now felt trivial. Sherri was busy with her last day at work, so I couldn't talk to her, and all the phone lines were jammed when I tried to call my parents.

Should I call off the closing? I wondered. *Should I still move to Arizona?*

Despite the turmoil, I knew I still needed to honor my commitment to sell my home, so I hurried to my attorney's office, where I got everything signed and handed over my condo keys. Then I waited in Sherri's office parking lot for her. I listened to the radio in our yellow moving truck with Daylie in the passenger seat, wanting to hear the latest news on the attacks. The broadcast announced the FAA had grounded all flights. I lived under a major route for flights leaving O'Hare International Airport, and the lack of air traffic, traffic that felt as normal to me as chirping birds, was unnerving.

Once Sherri was beside me in the truck, I felt relief to be leaving the Chicago area. I reasoned the iconic skyscrapers in an international city like Chicago would be more of a target than the suburban-like landscape of the Phoenix Metro Area. It was one thing that made leaving town on one of the darkest days of my life easier.

We arrived at our new home in the East Valley of Phoenix three days later. I was still in a fog. I'd lost the excitement I'd felt about starting my new life with Sherri in Phoenix the moment I turned on the news to see the World Trade Center's North Tower was on fire. It had been replaced with grief. I mourned the innocent lives lost and families affected by the tragic events of 9/11. I was starting a new normal I had no desire for.

Chapter 24

Flights resumed a week after Sherri and I arrived in Arizona. Coverage of 9/11 was still on every TV network, day and night. Thinking about the events made me angry, sad, and anxious, so I engrossed myself in projects around the house. Our new home contained five bedrooms and three bathrooms in just under three thousand square feet. I had rooms to paint and carpets to steam clean—the carpets were full of cat hair from the previous owner, and Sherri was allergic to cats. A month later, we adopted a second dog, and Max, a black-and-tan mutt that looked like a short, fat German shepherd, joined our family.

As if that weren't hectic enough, I started working for a new company just before Halloween and we built a pool in our backyard. Oh, and I turned thirty. It was a lot of firsts for a young couple months into their marriage, but Sherri and I navigated them together. By the time Christmas came around, I was ready to travel. I needed to fly or drive somewhere again.

We'd been planning to take our honeymoon on our first anniversary, but the world had changed dramatically since we made that decision. In the weeks after 9/11, Sherri was reluctant to travel overseas, and I wasn't convinced it was safe to push for it. However, once the calendar turned to 2002, Sherri told me she believed we could travel safely and I should book the trip. So I started on plans for our first international trip together—to the French Riviera and the Italian Riviera.

A European vacation with my new bride would be a trip different from the kind I was used to planning. I had three story-worthy adventures with friends under my belt, but I was ready for a new type of travel. Instead of targeting the best bars or clubs in whirlwind stops, I wanted to generate lasting memories with my wife. I was planning for something I loved with the person I loved. I wanted this to be a trip neither one of us would ever forget.

I chose to start in Nice, France, because I'd been planning to see it during my first trip to Europe but hadn't been able to because of the train strike. Also, the pictures I viewed online of the city built into the mountains along the Mediterranean Sea reminded me of Santa Barbara. After building several spreadsheets to analyze our options, I booked two nights in Nice and one night in Cannes, France. Next, I selected a hotel right on the sea in Santa Margherita Ligure, Italy. I'd liked numerous places during my trip eight years earlier, but this picturesque hamlet forty miles east of Genoa had ascended to true-love status. I wanted to share this experience with Sherri, so I reserved a room for two nights. Next, I booked flights for us into and out of Paris and found the perfect hotel in the Latin Quarter, just off Boulevard Saint-Michel, between the Luxembourg Gardens and the Fontaine Saint-Michel, near the Seine River. I finalized our itinerary and counted down the days.

One week before our first anniversary, Sherri and I boarded our flight destined for Paris for her first transatlantic flight. I used miles I'd accumulated from frequent business travel before 9/11 to bump us up to business class. Somewhere off the coast of Newfoundland, Sherri turned to me. "This isn't so bad. I thought you said the flight to Europe was pretty tough."

"Try flying in the middle seat in coach and see if you feel the same way."

"This isn't coach?"

I chuckled. "No, honey, this is business class. All the people in the back behind the curtain are crammed together with the goats and the chickens."

Sherri laughed. "Really? I just thought the planes flying over the ocean had more legroom."

"Go to the bathroom back there and see for yourself."

Minutes later, Sherri returned with a stunned look on her face. "Oh my gosh, you're right. There are like twenty people in a row back there."

"You better behave, or you'll be back there on the flight home," I exclaimed with a wide grin, which earned me a slap on the arm.

I thought it was cute she'd believed everyone traveled business class to Europe. Part of me felt she should have to fly coach across the pond as a rite of passage, but it was our anniversary, so I gave her a pass.

We landed at Charles de Gaulle International Airport the next morning after another sleepless flight, secured our luggage, cleared customs, and took a cab to our hotel in the Latin Quarter. The room was small by American standards but quaint. At least we had our own private bathroom, which was a requirement for Sherri. We took quick showers and rushed out to start exploring.

The neighborhood looked even more French than I'd pictured. The boulevard outside the hotel entrance was lined with restaurants, shops, and cafés below four- or five-story lofts. Some young people sat outside sipping drinks, while others strutted down the boulevard as though it were a catwalk.

Sherri and I moseyed down the boulevard and stopped every few steps to gawk at the goodies through the windows, the steel-blue French sky in the background of our reflections. The smells of freshly ground coffee and sweet syrups combined with that of the blooming flowers and trees heightened my senses. We stopped at an outdoor café for lunch, where I destroyed my baguette with ham and brie as if I hadn't eaten in days. It felt great to be back in Europe. I was content and more relaxed than I'd been in ages. We watched people walk by until we were ready to continue thirty minutes later.

We perused more stores and shops until we made it to the bridge over the Seine River and the pavilion outside Notre-Dame. The cathedral looked grander and more beautiful than I'd remembered. I suspect it was because last time I was trying to visit as many sights as possible in a day. This time, at a slower pace, I noticed the intricate details of each gargoyle, the color of the roof tiles, and the way the light hit the floor inside the cathedral.

Sherri and I then strolled down several cobblestone streets near our hotel and shopped in cramped stores too cute not to shell out euros by the fistful in. When it started to drizzle, we enjoyed dinner indoors at a proper French restaurant. Finally, the adrenaline wore off and tiredness took hold, so we crashed for the night.

After sleeping in and enjoying lunch near the hotel, we took the subway to the Eiffel Tower. I crossed under the same trees in the Champ-de-Mars I had eight years earlier, and like the Notre Dame Cathedral, it seemed more magnificent than last time. Slowing down to soak up all the features and minor details changed my perspective and my experience of Paris.

When we reached the fence at the top of the Eiffel Tower, I felt as if I were seeing Paris for the first time again. It hadn't changed much since my last visit eight years earlier, but I was wiser with more appreciation for what I saw on the streets below. Sherri and I separated to snap pictures and explore the city from one thousand feet above the streets. I pushed my face against the metal fence. Spotting people debarking from a boat along the Seine, I grinned. I couldn't wait for our next activity.

Back on the ground, we explored more shops and made our way to the river, where I surprised Sherri with tickets for a romantic sunset cruise. We ate dinner below deck and then found seats on the upper deck near the front. I pulled Sherri closer to me as the river-cruise vessel passed under bridges and long shadows of buildings. The slower pace kept revealing so much more of Paris to me—the blend of French Renaissance and classicism architecture intertwined with seductive cafes and charming shops. It was the perfect ending to a day in Paris.

The next morning, I found a neighborhood coffee shop filled with college-age patrons and a relaxed vibe. I sipped my coffee and watched the Parisians order their morning beverages while waiting for Sherri. This trip I felt less like an intruding tourist and more like a local getting his bearings after being away for too long. I was in my element, and I wanted to do everything possible for Sherri to share a similar experience.

When she was ready, we took a taxi to the train station and claimed our reserved seats on the TGV to Marseille. There would be no shared cabins or slow trains for my lady as we crossed the heart of France—only a high-speed train with comfortable bucket seats next to expansive windows would do.

Four hours and 450 miles later, we arrived in Marseille, where we changed trains. For this leg, our pace slowed from over 120 miles an hour to maybe 40 miles an hour with dozens of stops. The main train station in Nice finally appeared eight hours after we left Paris.

I'd reserved a hotel only a few blocks from the station, so we dragged our luggage down the street, checked in, and quickly changed clothes before bolting for the sea. I took Sherri's hand, and we walked along a pedestrian path parallel to Promenade des Anglais and the beaches of Nice until we reached the Promenade du Paillon and turned inland. The green grass and canopy of trees winding through the heart of Nice was a welcome respite from the sun. We snapped photos of the naked man with a crown at the Fountain of the Sun and headed farther into the interior.

By this time, we were starving, so we found a restaurant with outdoor seating along a lively shopping corridor. It allowed for the most sacred of French activities: people-watching. Sherri and I clinked our wine glasses in a toast to the beginning of our Riviera vacation.

Suddenly, out of the corner of my eye, I saw two men running through the street, and then I heard yelling. A half-dozen police officers caught up with the men and tackled them into tables of diners enjoying their meals on the other side of the narrow plaza. Patrons screamed and ran from the scene. I stood, and the hair on my neck did the same. The police had the two men under control and in custody in seconds, but it felt much longer. Sherri was also standing when I turned back to the table. We didn't have to say anything—our expressions spoke volumes. I'd let my guard down since I was no longer in the country of the 9/11 attacks. It was a stark reminder we no longer felt as safe as we had nine months earlier.

We ate our meals quickly and quietly and returned to our hotel several blocks away. It had been a long day, and I was tired both physically and mentally. The slim double bed in that room never felt so good.

Chapter 25

The next day, Sherri and I were in the mood for something a little slower and less urban—Nice has nearly one million residents and is the seventh-largest metro area in France—so we purchased tickets for a guided van tour of Monaco and some of the smaller hamlets along the route to the sovereign city-state. We boarded the blue tour van with two other couples, a male driver, and a female guide, who sat in the front passenger seat.

Our driver headed east out of Nice, and we drove past homes and businesses built into the hills until we dropped onto Napoleon Boulevard in the neighboring community of Villefranche-sur-Mer, with views of the picturesque harbor. Yachts and cruise ships danced around each other on the calm water, a kaleidoscope of light and dark blues. The driver pulled over at a scenic overview so we could get pictures of the French Riviera that looked like those featured in all the travel magazines.

Next, the van climbed back into the mountains until we reached Eze, France, a small medieval village built into the side of the cliffs. The driver was fortunate enough to find one of the limited parking spots and instructed us to be back at the van in one hour. The guide told us we'd reach an area with breathtaking views if we followed the cobblestone path to the bottom.

Sherri and I started down the pedestrian-only route and passed restaurants, galleries, and even individual homes situated within the cliff fortress. We walked through tunnels, marched down stairs, and meandered along tight corridors with lipstick-red bougainvillea shrubs and vines clinging to two-thousand-year-old stone walls, and when we reached the bottom of the path, just as our guide had said, we found an area with a superb view of the Mediterranean Sea. I gazed out at choppy water almost the same blue as the sky. I squinted and turned around to take in the village perched over the bay like an eagle's nest, hoping I could see it as it was one-thousand years earlier. I wasn't that lucky, but it was clear anyone who claimed Eze as their home was very fortunate.

Sherri and I took several pictures before I checked my watch and realized we had thirty minutes to climb all those stairs we'd descended. We hustled back.

I'd never heard of Eze before the van pulled in, but it was one of the most beautiful and interesting villages I'd visited in Europe.

The van headed east for another thirty minutes and stopped in front of the famous casino in Monte-Carlo, in the Principality of Monaco. I felt it was only appropriate to donate to the prosperous community inside the casino, and fifteen minutes later, I exited without all those pesky euros weighing me down. Sherri and I walked around the meticulous grounds in front of the casino until we found a street full of shops hoping for prospective customers with far more money than we had to spend.

After touring the casino area, we met up with the group again and made the short drive to the Palace of Monaco. The line for the indoor tour was too long, so we walked the grounds of royalty and took pictures of yachts parked in the harbor. We stood at the railing overlooking the collision of manmade beauty with the natural beauty of the landscape supporting it. I was in awe.

Later that afternoon, we returned to Nice. We were too tired from hiking Eze and exploring Monte-Carlo to walk any farther. Plus, our train to Italy left early the next morning, and we wanted to be well-rested for the Italian leg of our trip, so we ate dinner at a café near our hotel and went to bed.

The train pulled into Santa Margherita after lunch the following day, and Sherri and I made the same trek down the hill as Scott and I eight years earlier. The familiar view of the rooftops and the indigo sea put a little hop in my step.

Once we reached the harbor, we turned and walked several blocks alongside the shoreline until we reached our hotel. After checking in, we explored the pebbly beach across the street from our hotel and headed back to the central plaza near the statue of Santa Margherita I visited with Scott in 1994. When it was time for dinner, I scanned all the buildings next to Liberty Plaza until I found one that looked familiar. I pulled Sherri to the menu in the window and inspected it.

Would I be able to keep the promise I'd made to myself eight years earlier?

The menu looked familiar, and then I spotted it—the item that was part of the reason I'd flown six thousand miles back to Europe. I was about to enjoy the world's best calzone for the first time since 1994.

I ordered it with great enthusiasm and watched our server closely as he set it on the table in front of me. Fresh mozzarella and thick prosciutto burst from the flaky crust with one slice of my knife. I didn't speak while I savored every bite—it was as good as I'd remembered. I hope I'm able to repeat this experience for a third time later in life. Sherri also enjoyed her fresh catch of the day.

After dinner, we made the fifteen-minute trek back to our hotel. We planned to eat breakfast in the hotel and take a trolley to one of my top destinations on this trip for lunch the next day—Portofino. Although it was only a little past nine, we wanted to get an early start, so we went to bed. Just before we turned in, I found the switch to lower the metal shade outside our window. It was pitch black inside when I crawled into bed.

At one point, I woke up to go to the bathroom. After bumping into a table and chair getting back into bed in the dark room, I looked at the clock and frowned. It read 10:45. I couldn't believe I felt so rested after only ninety minutes of sleep. It wasn't until I lay back down that I noticed a thin beam of light coming from a pinhole in the metal shade. I opened it, and sunlight flooded the room. For several seconds I blinked in confusion. Then it hit me—we'd slept for thirteen hours. We'd missed breakfast, and we'd miss lunch in Portofino if we didn't leave soon. I woke Sherri, and she went through the same stages of confusion and panic.

We caught the eleven-thirty trolley to Portofino, and during the bouncy fifteen-minute ride, each of us must have said "I can't believe we slept thirteen hours" a hundred times. It's still the longest I've ever slept, and to this day Sherri talks about it with envy in her voice.

Portofino was more impressive than I'd imagined based on the pictures I'd viewed online. It was a tiny village, but it made up for its diminutive size with character and charm. High-end shops and restaurants mingled with pastel-colored homes to frame the harbor, which was lined with a motley crew of superyachts and local fishing boats. Despite the pewter sky and the threat of rain, we selected an outdoor café on the cobbled Piazzetta, the square overlooking the quiet harbor. After I'd polished off my delectable panini, we climbed the stairs to the Castello di San Giorgio overlooking Portofino. At the top, we were at eye level with the homes built into the side of the hill just above the Piazzetta. Here, the full majesty of Portofino unfurled like a scroll.

Now I understand why people with enough money to go anywhere in the world choose to visit Portofino. It was the ideal balance of old-world charm, stunning scenery, and modern hospitality. I loved everything about it.

A little after seven that evening, Sherri and I walked back to the central plaza in Santa Margherita to beat the local dinner rush. The weather had cleared, so we found a restaurant with an outdoor table overlooking the harbor. I ordered the fish special, swirled the white wine in my glass, and turned to the sea.

As the sun turned the water into swaths of gold and purple, I relaxed, and my mind drifted. For the second time in less than a decade, I felt at home in Santa Margherita. Memories of Vienna, Munich, Rome, and Prague wandered through my thoughts. I liked the beach, I liked the mountains, I liked the city, I liked the forest—but I loved with all my heart to stand where history had been made hundreds or thousands of years before me. Europe provided all of that, and I didn't want to let it go.

"I could live here," I said. "I think we should look into moving here."

Sherri just smiled and continued to watch the light show on the surface of the sea.

"What do you think?"

"Do you want to get any dessert? I bet the gelato is excellent."

I took the redirect as a no—or at least her attempt to wait out my delusion—so I softened my pitch. "Okay, maybe not permanently, but perhaps we could live over here for a year or two at a time? At a minimum, I'd want to spend my summers here."

"Really?" She looked at me. "I like it here too, but isn't living here full time a big jump?"

I felt my long-lost and newly rediscovered dream of living in Europe slipping through my fingers like sand. I switched gears again. I wasn't going down without a fight.

"Summers are the perfect time to come to Europe. It's more expensive, but the weather is perfect—summer is the worst time to be in Phoenix. Instead of heading to California like everyone else, we could come to Europe instead."

Sherri's eyebrows pinched together, and her nose wrinkled. "I thought we agreed to start a family, though. I don't want to be flying ten hours across an ocean with babies or toddlers. Plus, it's expensive, and you only get two weeks of vacation, so I don't know how that would even be possible."

I sighed. She was right. My dream was well-suited for a single person or a retiree, but not a young family. My desire to be a good husband and father was stronger than my desire to travel. Was it time to set aside this silly dream and face reality? Would this be my last trip across the pond?

I knew the answer but couldn't find my voice, so I turned to face the salty air drifting over the harbor. I wanted to remember every minute of my last night in Italy.

"Summers over here would be perfect when we retire," Sherri said, breaking the silence.

"When we retire?" I asked, to confirm and let my mind reengage.

"Yeah, once the kids are out of the house, we could spend a few months over here every summer to get out of the heat in Phoenix."

Bingo!

It wasn't raising my kids on the hills of Santa Margherita or Prague, but it was a good plan. It was also realistic. My mind raced with opportunities. "Yeah! We could visit a different city every year and rent a small house or apartment for three months, to get us out of the worst of the summer heat in Phoenix."

Sherri nodded.

I warmed quickly to the idea. I'd have to delay my gratification for over thirty years, but that would give me an incentive to work hard so I could retire early. It would also give me plenty of time to plan for the most epic travel schedule in the history of humankind.

"Some years we could stay in a big city, like Rome or Paris," I said excitedly, "and other years we could stay in a small village in Spain, to experience all aspects of living in Europe."

"That would be cool," Sherri replied with a smile.

Those four words became the new North Star that would guide my adult life. I pulled Sherri close, and we watched the sky turn from gold to blue to black with twinkling stars. I had a plan to make my dream a reality, and Sherri was a partner in this dream. Now it was a complete dream, and I was determined to fulfill it.

Chapter 26

I turned to scan Santa Margherita Ligure one last time before we entered the train station. I inhaled deeply, closed my eyes, and took a picture in my mind. I can still see that seaside village clearly today.

Three hours later, we arrived in Cannes, France. We wanted to break up the long journey back to Paris. Our hotel was a few blocks from the old port, and after checking in, we wandered down Alles de la Liberte Charles de Gaulle. Rows of pollarded plane trees surrounded us as we strolled the short street adjacent to the harbor. At first, I thought the trees—which were mostly trunk and branches with softball-size clumps of leaves—were late in blooming that season, but I learned the plane trees were pruned this way to generate the signature look of the Riviera dating back centuries. We walked the same boulevard the directors and actors attending the famous film festival would strut along one week after we departed.

Another early morning and cross-country train ride on the TGV later, we were back in Paris. On our last night in Europe, we found several pedestrian-only streets across the Seine from Notre-Dame and wandered up and down them gawking at bakeries with their sweets in the window. Near dinnertime, an inviting café caught our eye, and we ate our last meal in Paris on the eve of our one-year anniversary.

I was pensive as I swirled the white wine in my glass and watched Sherri take the last bites of her meal. This vacation to Europe was only eight days, but it felt longer and more fulfilling than previous, longer trips. Part of it was that I was accompanied by my bride of one year, but a bigger reason was the pace. Instead of barreling through countries to get a quick taste, Sherri and I took our time and savored every moment in France and Italy. It's how I'd like to visit Europe again on future trips. I just wished I didn't have to fly home yet. I could have stayed for another month.

Early the next morning, we wished each other a happy anniversary and embarked on our thirteen-hour trip to Sky Harbor International Airport in Phoenix, which included a connecting flight in Washington, DC. We told everyone it was our anniversary during our flight, including the flight attendant, which prompted her to bring us each a complimentary glass of wine. We joked about how we'd spent our first anniversary forty thousand feet in the air.

Back home, though, I noticed our picture book from our wedding with the date engraved on the front. Our anniversary had been the day before, while we were still in Paris. My heart sank. Was this a bad omen? I'd forgotten the date of our wedding on our first anniversary. Our first anniversary! But when I told Sherri, instead of getting angry, she bent over with laughter, so I joined her. For the next five minutes, we laughed about how we'd both forgotten the date. We're made for each other.

Sherri and I developed our pictures and shared them with friends and family, but we didn't discuss our future travel plans much. I still had many places on my wish list, but starting a family was the dominant conversation now. I was ready for the next adventure in my life—fatherhood.

When I'd accepted becoming the best father I can be to my future children was my number one priority, I believed my dreams of international travel and taking care of my family couldn't coexist—and to a certain extent, that was true. I couldn't do both the way I'd originally envisioned. As I begrudgingly accepted this new reality after our last trip to Europe, I had an epiphany. Dreams don't have to be binary—black or white; win or lose. I could retain my international travel goals by reshaping them. The timing and length of each stay would have to change, but the core premise could remain intact. Extended tours of months or years across the pond were not feasible, but a week here and a couple weeks there were certainly within reason, even for a family with small children. I knew it was possible, and that was all I needed to keep the dream burning inside me.

Even though starting a family was our priority, I continued to research future destinations and often shared pictures of the idyllic-looking towns in Spain, France, Germany, and Italy with Sherri that I was adding to my growing post-retirement wish list. I told her to imagine the two of us lounging with our morning coffee and tea at bistro tables and then strolling down to the market to buy fresh produce and cheese. We'd explore the area until the stars came out and then return to our balcony overlooking the town square and drink red wine from a local vineyard. I was constantly selling her on the idea of returning to Europe with kids in the nearer term and as retirees in the long-term. I had her on the hook, and I didn't want her to slip off. Ever.

The Continent will always have a special allure for me. Though the idea is romanticized in media, Europe does have an energy unlike any other on the planet. I'm also aware it has its share of problems, though. I saw the homelessness and the substance abuse in the streets, along with various political and cultural divisions—issues we know all too well in the US.

My international travels have taken me to Malaysia, Singapore, Canada, and Mexico, and I liked all these places, but they didn't feel the same as Europe. In Europe, even mundane tasks were appealing to me. Getting groceries was fun. Eating at McDonald's was fun. Shopping for flip-flops was fun. I'm sure that would wear off if I lived there full-time, but the joy exists in short bursts, and that's how I intend to consume Europe. One small bite at a time.

I've come a long way from believing my tiny hometown in Central Illinois could offer all I'd ever want or need in life. Traveling sharpened my practice of empathy. It started in the military when I was first immersed in a diverse environment and grew stronger every time I took a trip that required a passport. When you meet people from different geographies, backgrounds, religions, and worldviews and truly get to know them, they are no longer nameless nouns. Instead, they become "real people" and feel more similar than different. Countries are no longer just colorful shapes on a map or another word on the teleprompter for the news anchor. Countries are full of people. People who have families, friends, and neighbors. People who have basic wants and needs, just like my friends, family, and neighbors. People that smile when they are happy, cry when they are sad, and laugh when someone walks into a closed glass door, just like we do. They are no longer just statistics, no longer simply Germans or Italians. They are Christian, Boris, Arndt, Veronika, and Luciana. They are billions of other people I don't know.

I'm forever grateful for watching the Berlin Wall come down on TV, studying WWII in high school history, Army basic training, German class in college, the study abroad program, the fish dinner in Malaysia, and everyone who sat beside me on an international flight. Each of those experiences helped me understand the importance of empathy for all people and I'm a better person today because of it.

Chapter 27

Two years after we moved to Arizona, Sherri surprised me with an invitation to meet me during my lunch break. She didn't make the thirty-mile drive to my office often, so I was excited to request a table for two instead of the typical party of one at a nearby restaurant. After some small talk and half my kung pao chicken, I noticed Sherri kept smiling.

"What's going on?" I asked. "You're all giddy about something. What is it?"

"I'm pregnant."

My jaw dropped. "Really? Are you sure?"

"Yep. We're having a baby in eight months."

A thousand thoughts flashed through my mind in less than a second. Fear, doubt, relief, delight, primal manliness but most of all—excitement.

I jumped up and hugged Sherri. I was going to be a father!

My next adventure was about to begin, and I couldn't wait. The old dream of living or traveling abroad would become new again once I retired, and I was confident it would be worth the wait. I now found myself looking at two horizons. One was close enough to touch; the other was barely visible in the distance, but it was always there, just above the arc of land.

With a smile, I focused my gaze on the closer horizon. I had important things to think about, such as raising my child to avoid making the same mistakes I'd made and giving them rich experiences that would help them determine their values, beliefs, passions, and dreams. I wanted my kid to find horizons worth chasing.

And perhaps we'd chase a few together. As a family.

* * *

Receive updates about Robert Goluba's new releases, promotions, and original stories, in a monthly email newsletter. Sign up now at RoberGoluba.com/newsletter

About Author

Robert Goluba is an author of thrillers, suspense, and memoir. He was born and raised in Central Illinois, where he attended college, served in the Army National Guard, and met his wife. At age thirty, after a self-diagnosed allergy to snow, he moved to sunny Arizona where he now lives with his wonderful wife, two kids, and canine companion.

He's published four books in the Dangerous Redemption Christian Suspense Collection, **Absolute Command** (Prequel), **Inviting Danger** (Book 1), **Last Second Chance** (Book 2), and **A Final Thread** (Book 3).
   Two Horizons: A memoir of Travel and Transformation is his first memoir.
   He loves to travel, spend time outdoors, watch football, and annoy his teenage daughters with his dad jokes.

Visit **RobertGoluba.com** to learn more.

www.ingramcontent.com/pod-product-compliance
Lightning Source LLC
Chambersburg PA
CBHW060355080526
44583CB00012B/318